CHATHAM HOUSE PAPERS · 35

DEVELOPING COUNTRY DEBT

CHATHAM HOUSE PAPERS · 35

DEVELOPING COUNTRY DEBT

THE ROLE OF THE COMMERCIAL BANKS

H. A. Holley

The Royal Institute of International Affairs

Routledge & Kegan Paul
London, New York and Andover

This paper forms part of the Institute's international economic programme.

The Royal Institute of International Affairs is an unofficial body which promotes the scientific study of international questions and does not express opinions of its own. The opinions expressed in this publication are the responsibility of the author

First published 1987
by Routledge & Kegan Paul Ltd
11 New Fetter Lane, London EC4P 4EE
29 West 35th Street, New York, NY 10001, USA, and
North Way, Andover, Hants SP10 5BE

Reproduced from copy supplied by
Stephen Austin and Sons Ltd
Printed in Great Britain by
Redwood Burn Limited
Trowbridge, Wiltshire

Library of Congress Cataloging-in-Publication Data

Holley, H.A., 1924-
    Developing country debt.

    (Chatham House papers ; 35)
    Bibliography: p.
    1. Loans, Foreign – Developing countries.
2. Debts, External – Developing countries.
3. Banks and banking, International.   I. Title.
II. Series: Chatham House papers : no. 35.
HG3891.5.H65   1987   336.3'435'091724   86-29838

ISBN 0-7102-1211-9

CONTENTS

ACKNOWLEDGMENTS

The author is grateful to former colleagues and to many others in banking and official organizations on both sides of the Atlantic who gave up valuable time to discuss the developing country debt problem and related issues. Their specialist knowledge was invaluable. Thanks are due also to the members of a study group, held at Chatham House, who read the paper in draft and who made many helpful comments. Needless to say, all views expressed in this paper are to be attributed solely to the author, as are any errors of fact or interpretation. Particular mention must be made of the help given by Joan Pearce, formerly of Chatham House, in organizing the study group, and by Pauline Wickham, whose patience and editorial skill put in order a somewhat disorderly text.

January 1987   H.A.H.

1

THE HISTORICAL PERSPECTIVE

Whatever the precedents in the long history of international lending and investment, the developing country debt crisis that erupted in 1982 is in many ways unique, and not least in the volume of comment and analysis that it has already received. Its uniqueness stems in large part from its systemic implications. The world economic crisis of the 1930s, to which many commentators have looked back in search of a parallel, had a devastating impact on the developing countries and involved widespread defaults, but the debt of those countries – painful though the losses inflicted on investors were – constituted no threat to the world economic system. It was the breakdown in economic relationships between the industrial countries themselves that was then the real problem. The essential reason why the developing country debt crisis of the 1980s, unlike that of the 1930s, had systemic implications lies in the nature and scale of the involvement of the international banks.

Scope of the study
In the few years since the crisis broke, much has been achieved. Most of the leading banks in the principal financial centres were heavily involved in lending to the developing countries, and the threat to the stability of the international banking system, which appeared very real when so many countries simultaneously failed to meet their obligations, has been defused if not eliminated. Mechanisms for dealing with the debtors' immediate liquidity problems have been devised and implemented. More recently, the parties involved have

begun to look beyond crisis management to a more constructive approach that takes into account the longer-term aims of economic policy. However, nothing that could appropriately be called a 'solution' to the problem of developing country debt is in sight: the original debt in nearly every case remains outstanding, and for most borrower countries it has tended to increase; for many of them, its existence constitutes a major constraint on economic policy. For the principal lending banks, and for their regulators, the dangers arising from loans of doubtful quality have been attenuated, but remain an element of weakness in bank balance-sheets. There are also wider implications: governments of industrialized countries are directly involved, both as lenders or guarantors of loans to the problem debtor countries and through their responsibilities to the multi-lateral financial organizations; and they cannot ignore the political dimension of the intractable economic problems of debtor countries.

The present study, being essentially concerned with the problems arising from bank debt, has little to say on the debt and related development-finance problems of the many developing countries, particularly in Africa and Asia, that for various reasons have borrowed little from the banks. Many of these countries face grave economic problems, but neither individually nor collectively do their debts constitute a problem for the lenders. The study focuses on the problems of fifteen major bank-debtor countries* – mainly in Latin America and variously described as the 'heavily indebted countries', in the terminology of the International Monetary Fund (IMF), or as the fifteen 'Baker Plan' countries – but it also looks at the position of some other bank borrowers, including those in Eastern Europe.

The greatly expanded role of the international commercial banks in developing country finance from the early 1970s onwards was so unusual that it is worth looking at the previously well-established pattern of external finance – a pattern to which the system appears gradually to be reverting. This paper therefore begins by briefly considering the traditional role of the international commercial banks in financing the developing countries, the new elements in postwar financing, and the factors and mechanisms in the international currency and capital markets that made it possible for banks to play the key role in the process of 'recycling' to deficit countries

---

*Argentina, Bolivia, Brazil, Chile, Colombia, Ivory Coast, Ecuador, Mexico, Morocco, Nigeria, Peru, Philippines, Uruguay, Venezuela and Yugoslavia.

the huge surpluses created by the successive rises in the price of oil in the 1970s. The destabilizing effect of these oil-price increases was of course one of the principal factors in the accumulation of bank debt by developing countries and, at one remove, in the world recession of the 1980s that so greatly intensified the problem. Some attention is given to the question – still not easy to answer satisfactorily – why a crisis of such magnitude was not foreseen.

Subsequent themes are the evolution of procedures and techniques whereby banks and debtor countries came to agreement on the terms of rescheduling or restructuring debt, the role of the IMF, the effort of economic adjustment required from rescheduling countries and the strains and resentments to which it gave rise, leading to the new approach linked with the name of the US Secretary of the Treasury, James Baker. Because this new approach ascribes a larger role to the multilateral development agencies, the relevance of their activities to the debt problem is given some consideration, along with the role of OECD governments as providers of finance. The latter are also important because, in a more general sense, their economic, financial and trading policies will largely determine the environment in which the continuing debt problem must be kept under control. The study further examines the current interests of the lending banks and of the debtor countries – sometimes coincident, sometimes conflicting – in a domestic and international financial environment that has been changing over the last four years. In conclusion, it looks at the key issues around which discussion of the debt problem must revolve. Rather than put forward any general solution – and indeed the author would claim that no 'solution', in practical as opposed to academic terms, is to be expected – it considers what might be done to make an unsatisfactory situation more tolerable.

The first question is how and why the commercial banks became involved in lending to countries of the developing world on a scale that was without historical precedent.

The pattern of postwar lending

Commercial banks based in the United Kingdom, the USA and other industrial states were historically important in financing the developing countries, but only in some quite specific ways: by the establishment from the mid-nineteenth century onwards of branches

3

in their chief commercial centres and the consequent introduction into these countries of modern banking practices, and by the provision of short-term trade finance for exports and imports and foreign-exchange facilities. They also financed domestic trade and provided short-term working capital for local enterprises; they rarely became involved in longer-term finance for domestic customers, and those that did so had more often than not cause to regret the fact, as the history of European banking in Latin America well illustrates. Long-term finance for capital projects, whether in industry or in the economic infrastructure, was provided by private investors, and it was merchant banks rather than commercial banks that acted as intermediaries. Development finance, as it would be defined nowadays, was for the risk-takers, who made direct investments of equity capital, or for bondholders, who subscribed to national and provincial government or public utility loans. When, as happened sporadically during the nineteenth century and more generally in the 1930s, these investments failed to produce a return (in the case of equity capital), or when bond issues fell into default (as happened at some time with every Latin American borrowing country and in many other parts of the world), the loss fell upon private individuals.

The losses experienced by investors in the 1930s effectively closed foreign bond markets to Latin American borrowers for a generation; for most developing countries, bond issues have not since then been a significant source of external finance. In the changed economic and political climate following the Second World War, official – i.e. government-administered on the lending side – finance became for many developing countries the main source of external funds. From a mixture of motives, the industrial countries in the OECD accepted a role in development finance, both bilaterally through aid for the poorest countries and generally through the provision, or more often the guaranteeing and perhaps subsidizing, of export finance, and multilaterally through the Bretton Woods institutions – the World Bank and its affiliates – and the subsequently established regional development banks. Private capital flows during this period consisted mainly of direct investment, which continued to play an important part in developing country finance, though one that was constrained by the often ambivalent attitudes of host countries. The role of the banks remained much as it had been: the provision of short-term finance through overseas branches and correspondent bank networks. As medium-term finance for capital goods exports grew increasingly important, the banks became involved in this sort of lending, with the support of official export-credit mechanisms, and often also provided associated unguaranteed credit. They also made medium-term loans in support of customers with activities in developing countries, especially those multinational corporate customers with whom they aimed to build up a world-wide relationship. With the growth of world trade and general economic expansion, such business increased, but overall cross-border lending by banks was a small part of their assets and a small, if growing, part of the external finance of developing countries.

The relative importance of different sources of finance, as it was before the great expansion of commercial bank lending in the 1970s and as it has since evolved, is shown in Table 1.

Table 1 Net financial flows to developing countries, 1960–85 (percentage shares)

	1960–1	1970	1975	1980	1985
Official development finance					
of which:	59	46	45	35	60
DAC bilateral aid	48	28	14	14	28
OPEC bilateral aid	—	2	10	7	3
Multilateral aid	2	5	7	6	9
Multilateral non-					
concessional lending	2	3	4	4	11
Export credits	14	13	10	13	4
Private flows	27	41	45	51	36
of which:					
Direct investment	19	18	20	9	10
Bank sector	6	15	21	38	16
Bonds	—	2	1	1	5

Source: OECD, *Financing and External Debt of Developing Countries: 1985 Survey* (Paris, 1986), p.9.

The eurocurrency markets
The increasingly important role of the commercial banks in developing country finance that characterized the 1970s was not solely the consequence of the OPEC-induced oil-price shocks. The evolution of their business in the same direction had already begun in the late 1960s and would no doubt in any case have continued to develop, though on nothing like so large a scale. The instruments for bank lending described below were as applicable to the needs of developing country borrowers as to those of the large private-sector corporations and public-sector agencies in the industrial countries themselves. Indeed, one of the first recorded loan syndications was made in 1969 to a developing country borrower, Iran. Given the deficiencies in size and flexibility of local capital markets in developing countries, it was perfectly natural that creditworthy borrowers in those countries should seek medium-term finance abroad. The 15 per cent of total financial flows to developing countries in 1970 attributed to banks in Table 1 represented net lending of about US$3bn; by 1973, already some US$7bn of syndicated loans (not of course the same as *net* financial flows) were arranged for developing country borrowers on the international markets. Conditions in the early 1970s were particularly favourable, since the developed countries were experiencing a remarkably coincident economic upswing – in a sense the culmination of the halcyon period of 25 years' uninterrupted growth that the world had enjoyed since the end of the Second World War, and the benefits spilled over to the developing countries, whose creditworthiness was enhanced by high commodity prices.

This lending took place largely through the eurocurrency markets. The establishment in London in the late 1950s of a market in non-resident dollar deposits may be seen, together with the restoration of convertibility in Europe, as the first step in the integration of world financial markets that has continued with accelerating pace up to the mid-1980s. The relative degree of freedom from control enjoyed by these markets in non-resident currencies – as against national credit and capital markets, where growth of bank credit was limited by reserve requirements and other constraints arising from domestic monetary policy, and where access to bond markets was limited so as to ensure access to long-term funds for domestic borrowers – gave them great flexibility and enabled banks operating in them to work on significantly narrower margins. In the 1970s the market became world-wide, 'euro'-dollar becoming a misnomer and the 'asian' dollar being nothing distinctive: it spanned the major financial capitals and an increasing number of 'offshore' centres. Exchange controls could insulate the domestic from the international financial market (as in the United Kingdom up to 1979), so that London, with the active encouragement of its regulatory authorities, retained its leading position, if with a gradually declining share of the total market.

London was in a sense the greatest of the offshore markets, attracting some 400 foreign banks, which came largely in order to participate in the euromarkets. These included an increasing number of banks from outside the OECD area, notably from the Middle East, the Far East and Latin America, which were eager to participate in loans to their home countries and adjacent states; the involvement of these banks was subsequently to create issues of some importance, especially in relation to money-market facilities, in the rescheduling processes of the 1980s. Banks in countries with fully convertible currencies could of course, and did, lend direct to foreign borrowers, but domestic monetary constraints often made it more profitable to operate through branches and subsidiaries abroad, as with German banks in Luxembourg. The USA was belatedly to permit the establishment of centres for offshore business within its own territory, the International Banking Facilities (IBFs), with the aim of bringing back some of the non-resident dollar business that had been lost to centres overseas.

The technical development of the late 1960s that made possible the large-scale mobilization of funds for eurocurrency borrowers was the syndicated roll-over credit. The banks protected themselves from interest-rate variations by lending at a margin over the cost of funds, determined at the end of each roll-over period (say, three or six months); the risk on the borrower was spread among many banks by the loan managers, who sold off participations in the loan. By these means the risk of lending was minimized for any one bank: costs were low, and the larger the loan the smaller they were in relation to the anticipated return. Management of syndicated loans brought in fees that were highly remunerative, and mandates from borrowers to act as lead manager or co-manager were eagerly sought after. The pages of the financial press carried advertisements – for the record only – of loan syndications, listing in strict order of precedence the managers and other participants, and known from their standard format as 'tombstones'. The specialist journals published league tables totalling quarter by quarter and year by year

7

the number of lead management and co-management positions won by the international banks.

Lead banks necessarily held part of the loans in their own portfolios, and it was a normal feature of the process that, just as they expected to place part of the loans they were managing with other major banks, so they themselves would reciprocate when the roles were reversed. Further down the scale were many banks – especially the numerous medium-sized and small banks in the USA, but also others in Europe – which did not themselves aspire to manage syndicated credits. These did not necessarily have much ability to gauge the quality of the loan, other than on the strength and expertise of the organizing bank, even though placement memoranda were always careful to state that participants should make their own independent decisions. For such banks with spare lending capacity, participation offered what appeared to be low-risk assets at minimal administrative cost. It was this process of 'selling down' loan participations that led to the vast increase in the number of banks – up to 700 in some cases – that had claims on debtor countries and had to be brought into the rescheduling process.

For such lucrative business the competition among leading banks was intense, and the market for syndicated credits grew rapidly; from the customers' point of view, borrowing on the euromarkets was relatively cheap, convenient and subject to little if any conditionality on the use of funds. The eurocurrency market was essentially demand-oriented: deposits in convertible currencies could always be bid for and obtained. In the period up to the onset of the debt crisis, the growth of the market suffered only one brief slippage of confidence. Despite warnings from academic economists on the dangers of erecting a pyramid of credit on a supposedly narrow base, the stability of the market was never really in question, even in 1974 when the collapse of the Herstatt bank, coincident with other banking problems in leading OECD countries, led to a temporary contraction of the inter-bank market.

Statistics on the size of the eurocurrency market with any pretension to comprehensiveness did not appear until about 1973, when the Bank for International Settlements (BIS) began to publish series that, with constant refinement, have remained the basic source of information on total bank cross-border exposure and the size of borrowing countries' debt to banks. Lending through the eurocurrency markets rose by an average of 25 per cent annually between

1973 and 1979. The total outstanding exceeded US$1,100bn in the latter year, of which about 60 per cent represented lending between the industrialized countries themselves; net of inter-bank lending, the size of the market was some 40 per cent smaller. The web of inter-bank lending was an important factor in ensuring the liquidity of the market, especially in view of the mismatch of maturities between deposits that were preponderantly at short term, while much lending under syndicated credits was in the 5-to-10-year range. The reasons for the growth of developing countries' involvement in the market as both lenders and borrowers are discussed in the following chapter.

2

THE ACCUMULATION
OF DEBT

The eurocurrency markets, operating in conditions of ample liquidity, provided the vehicle for a rapid expansion of bank lending to developing countries. The incentive to use these markets on the scale experienced from the mid-1970s onwards was provided by the disruptive influence on the balance of payments of most countries, both developed and developing, of successive OPEC-induced oil-price shocks and subsequently by the most radical change in monetary policy since the war in the principal OECD countries, led by the USA.

Of these disruptive elements, the first was the fourfold increase in the price of oil imposed by OPEC in 1973-4. Although the increase was in the event to be allowed to work rapidly through the economies of the industrial countries to produce unprecedented levels of price inflation, the real danger to the world economic system was at the time perceived to be not inflation but the deflation of demand as income was transferred from users in the oil-importing countries to governments in exporting countries, and particularly to the so-called 'low absorbers' like Saudi Arabia, Kuwait and other small Gulf states that could not spend on investment or immediate consumption more than a small part of their vastly increased revenues. The reaction in major OECD countries was therefore to accommodate the oil-price rise by encouraging the recycling of dollars that accrued to OPEC and would for the most part sit idly in foreign bank accounts: in other words, to finance the balance of payments of deficit countries. There were other considerations, too, that made accommodation rather than confrontation seem the most reasonable policy: the political situation in the Middle East was highly unstable, and the world economy was in any case in a cyclical downswing that made a new deflationary impulse seem particularly undesirable.

For the recycling of OPEC surpluses to deficit countries, both industrial and developing, the only vehicle of sufficient size, flexibility and speed of operation was the eurocurrency market, and there followed a rapid expansion of bank lending to public- and private-sector borrowers in both groups of countries. Although this process sowed the seeds of the debt crisis (and it could be argued that policies of adjustment then might have avoided the traumatic experiences of the 1980s), there is no evidence that the governments of OECD countries ever contemplated any collective action that went beyond consultation on oil policy, the establishment of oil reserves and the encouragement of a more economical use of fuel. That the recycling process and the commercial banks' key role in it was not only accepted but applauded by governments and international financial bodies may be seen in the political speeches of the time, in statements by central bank governors and by the executive director of the IMF, and in the annual reports of these institutions and of the BIS.[1] If the banks are to be criticized, it is not for their role in the recycling process of the 1970s but for continuing to lend on so large a scale in the early 1980s when the world economic environment had changed radically. But even at that later stage there is no evidence that they acted against the advice of their regulators or of the monitors of the international system. This does not of course absolve them from errors of judgment about the creditworthiness of developing country borrowers; the fact was that neither they nor the governments of OECD countries realized how far-reaching were to be the consequences of the change in industrial countries' monetary policies.

Implicit in the recycling process, however, was the virtual abandonment of the principle that bank lending should normally be related to some specified end-use; whatever the nominal public-sector borrower, most lending was providing general support for macroeconomic policy by financing budget and balance-of-payments deficits. This contrasted with the earlier period of cross-border financing, when loans were invariably linked to the import of capital goods, plus the financing of associated costs of investment or

11

a prudent extension of working capital facilities. The distinction between project finance and general-purpose lending was maintained by the larger international banks, which built up specialized project-finance departments whose function it was to put together financial packages – in one or several currencies – combining export credit, financing of associated local costs and perhaps also equity capital for major investments, especially in natural resource development. However, as the scale of developing country borrowing increased, and as public-sector borrowing was consolidated into larger loans, the proportion that was directly related to specific investment projects declined, and that part for which debt service was guaranteed by the earnings of a specific project was much smaller still. In the event, whatever the initial purpose of the loan, it went into the general pot of sovereign indebtedness. The position was no different in the case of developed country borrowers such as the United Kingdom, France and Italy, which generally preferred to conduct their external borrowing through their nationalized industries rather than under the name of the government itself.

The international commercial banks responded with vigour to the opportunities provided by the OPEC-induced deficits. The growth of bank lending to major developing country borrowers and groups is shown in Table 2. Bank lending to final (i.e. non-bank) borrowers, official and private, in other developed countries also expanded, but rather less rapidly: about 20 per cent a year between 1974 and 1982, against 24 per cent for loans to developing countries. As the banks' domestic business grew more slowly than foreign lending, the share of the latter in total bank claims rose from about 8 per cent at the end of 1974 to nearly 17 per cent by the end of 1982, while the share of lending to developing countries rose from 3 per cent to $7\frac{1}{2}$ per cent over the same period.[2]

Among the developing countries the oil importers borrowed to sustain economic growth; the 'high-absorbing' oil exporters borrowed in anticipation of future revenue. The banks regarded the latter as particularly desirable customers, notably Mexico, which as well as oil had a fairly well-diversified agricultural and industrial base. Some 120 banks set up representative offices in Mexico City for the purpose of arranging foreign currency business, as they were forbidden to engage in domestic banking operations. The pattern was repeated elsewhere: major international banks, mainly from the USA and the UK, but also Japanese, French and other European

Table 2 Growth of bank cross-border lending, 1977–82 (US$ bn, end-year)

Borrowing country	1977	1978	1979	1980	1981	1982
INDUSTRIAL COUNTRIES	405.4	531.5	660.7	790.2	920.3	1007.0
OFFSHORE CENTRES	98.2	125.4	157.4	188.8	238.2	267.9
EASTERN EUROPE	38.3	47.6	55.9	59.8	60.7	53.3
OPEC COUNTRIES	36.8	56.4	64.1	69.9	72.1	78.8
of which:						
Indonesia	4.1	4.5	4.2	4.3	4.5	6.2
Nigeria	0.7	1.8	2.5	3.4	4.7	7.0 ·
Venezuela	8.0	12.8	18.5	21.3	22.3	22.7
NON-OPEC DCs	97.2	119.9	155.7	193.3	229.6	247.2
Latin America	64.7	79.1	102.5	129.2	158.3	169.2
of which:						
Argentina	4.8	6.7	13.0	18.9	22.9	22.2
Brazil	23.8	31.7	36.8	43.3	49.6	56.1
Chile	1.6	2.7	4.5	6.7	9.6	10.4
Colombia	1.7	2.1	3.5	4.3	4.9	5.5
Mexico	19.9	23.3	30.8	41.0	55.3	58.9
Middle East	5.2	6.5	7.8	9.7	11.5	12.9
Africa	7.8	11.3	14.3	15.9	16.9	18.0
Asia	19.5	22.9	31.1	38.4	42.8	47.1
of which:						
S. Korea	6.0	6.9	10.3	14.0	16.9	18.8
Philippines	3.1	4.0	5.4	7.0	7.2	8.3
TOTAL (incl. international institutions and unallocated)	689.7	893.1	1111.0	1321.9	1549.5	1688.2

Source: BIS, *International Banking Developments*, Quarterly Series, various issues. Totals for 1977 are partly estimated.

banks, that already operated branch networks abroad – often for historical reasons concentrated in certain geographical areas – continued throughout the 1970s to extend them with the aim of establishing a world-wide coverage. Where, as in Mexico, local regulations prohibited the opening of bank branches or the acquisition of locally incorporated subsidiaries, they set up representative offices and made use of offshore banking centres in the Caribbean, the Middle East and Far East, through which regional foreign currency business could conveniently be handled.

The banks, through their regional and country lending offices, competed strongly for borrowers' mandates to manage loans. Although a number of exotic names such as Gabon and Angola appeared in the list of syndications, caution prevailed at an early stage in relation to the poorest countries. (North Korea provided an early example – fortunately on a small scale – of the dangers of lending to a country about whose economy little was known and whose competence to engage in responsible financial relations with the outside world was doubtful.) Among the developing country borrowers, therefore, the banks concentrated on those whose stage of development and degree of integration into the world system through trade and investment were deemed to give them the capacity to take on debt at market rates: these were the countries that the World Bank was to classify as 'middle-income developing countries' or 'commercial market borrowers'. They were located for the most part in Latin America, the Far East and the Mediterranean, with the addition both of one or two African states such as the Ivory Coast and of East European countries that lived outside the IMF/World Bank system. The multilateral and bilateral aid agencies were thus enabled to concentrate their efforts on the poor countries of Asia and Africa which could not afford to take on much debt at commercial terms.

Within the range of developing countries that were deemed creditworthy, the margins charged on loans over the cost of funds were related to risk only in a rather approximate sense. As the market became more competitive, periods of relative tightness became short and margins tended to decline over the whole range of borrowers, so that there could be as little as one-half of a percentage point between a prime developed country borrower such as Electricité de France and one of the larger Latin American countries. Margins were determined by the market and reflected the supply and demand for a country's paper and its attractiveness in building up a diversified portfolio; a loan for a new name among the sovereign borrowers might be saleable at a low margin because, and not in spite, of its unfamiliarity. The lower the margin, the more attractive the earning of management fees that enhanced the overall yield on the operation. Borrowers, for their part (and if they did not have the skills themselves, they could hire them), became adept at exploiting the competition for mandates and at taking advantage of refinancing opportunities when market conditions moved in the borrowers' favour. The refinancing of debt on more advantageous terms and at the borrower's option was normal before rescheduling became a necessity.

In so far as the policy of accommodation to the first oil-price shock aimed at maintaining world economic growth and trade, it may be accounted reasonably successful: the average annual increase in GNP in the developing countries between 1974 and 1979 was 5.6 per cent against 2.7 per cent in the OECD. Some countries ran into financial difficulties in the later 1970s which required banks to carry out debt-restructuring operations. These included the Indonesian state oil concern, Pertamina, in 1976, and subsequently Jamaica, Zaire, Turkey and Peru required renegotiation of commercial bank debts; but these, except for Turkey, were on a relatively small scale. They were not seen to cast any doubt upon lending to developing countries generally, but were regarded, rather, as assistance at a time of temporary balance-of-payments difficulty, analogous to the refinancing of export credits that had been arranged at various times, especially for Latin American borrowers, since 1956, through the mechanism of the 'Paris Club' of official export-credit agencies.

In 1979–80, however, the environment for international lending suffered two further shocks. In October 1979 the Federal Reserve announced a new stance in US monetary policy: alarmed at the persistence of inflationary pressures, the US authorities adopted monetary targets that, unlike previous vacillating efforts at monetary control, were to be pursued with determination, regardless of the effect on interest rates. By 1981 the reference rate for borrowers on the eurocurrency markets, the London Inter-Bank Offered Rate (LIBOR) peaked at about 19 per cent and averaged about 14 per cent in that year, some 7 percentage points above the average in 1978. The second shock was the artificially induced rise in oil prices which, though it brought about only an approximate doubling of average prices, was in dollar terms as large a shock to the world economy, and of course to the balance of payments of the oil importers, as the fourfold increase of 1973–4 had been. As other

OECD countries followed the same course as the USA and gave priority to economic adjustment rather than to accommodation, the cyclical downswing of the early 1980s became the worst recession for 50 years, and was rapidly transmitted to the developing countries through foreign trade, commodity prices and interest rates.[3]

Although the banks' perception of increased risk in international lending became sharper, bank debt of the capital-importing developing countries continued to rise during 1980–2 at an average of 16–17 per cent a year, though this was only about half the rate of 1979. Before the general crisis of late 1982, a number of specific problem cases emerged. Some of these, as with Nicaragua in 1979 and Poland in the following year, were political as much as economic in origin. In Nicaragua the bank debt was less than US$600m and the economy of the country had been ruined by civil war. Poland was a more serious case: political turmoil and a chaotic economic situation led in 1980 to the suspension of bank credit facilities, the accumulation of arrears of payments to both bank and official creditors (the latter held some 60 per cent of the total debt, a far higher proportion than with the other major debtors that were later to constitute the core of the debt problem) and long-drawn-out negotiations that lasted until the bank rescheduling agreement was reached in 1982, while political considerations were to delay negotiations with official creditors even longer. The amounts involved were much larger than in earlier reschedulings, about US$4.8bn for both classes of credit combined. Some 500 banks were involved in what was the first large-scale attempt at organizing the collective approach that was later, through ample experience, to be refined and standardized.

Although Poland was for political reasons a special case, some other countries in the area, notably Yugoslavia, found themselves cut off from new bank borrowing, and Eastern Europe – other than the USSR itself – came under general suspicion. More generally, a mood of caution began to make itself felt in lending quarters in 1981, and this was to deepen in the following year. A large volume of loan syndications continued to be arranged, including 'jumbo' operations of up to US$1bn, but the growth in net exposure of the banks to developing countries slowed down markedly. Since the established pattern of bank borrowing required new loans to be arranged in sufficient volume to cover both capital repayments and at least part of current balance-of-payments financing, and because the cushion of reserves was for most countries small, any interruption of the process was likely to create liquidity problems for the debtor. As the terms of lending hardened, many countries increased their short-term borrowing and made fuller use of trade credit and money market facilities. For individual lending banks, the shortening of terms could appear a prudent limitation of risk; it was not immediately apparent that, applied over the whole system, it signalled an approaching crisis point.

The onset of the debt crisis is usually dated from August 1982, when Mexico announced a moratorium on repayments and asked leading banks to form an advisory committee. But confidence in Latin America generally had been seriously eroded already; Argentina was in grave economic difficulties after the Falklands war and Brazil's position was scarcely tenable. Negotiations for one of the largest 'jumbo' loans to consolidate and refinance earlier borrowings of Venezuela had collapsed in mid-year because the parties were unable to agree on terms. By the end of 1982 some 20 countries had suspended payments, and the number rose to over 30 by the end of 1983. Their number included all the Latin American countries except Colombia, Paraguay, El Salvador and Nicaragua (which had already rescheduled); in Asia and Africa, the Philippines, Nigeria and Morocco were the only substantial debtor countries in a similar position, though many small African countries also fell into arrears; in Eastern Europe, Romania joined Poland and Yugoslavia; and another COMECON member, Cuba, was soon among the Latin American problem countries.

The assessment of creditworthiness

In retrospect it is easy to see that in the circumstances of the early 1980s the accumulation of debt, and especially bank debt, was rising towards a critical level for many, if not all, the countries that were eventually forced to reschedule. Whether a general crisis might have been averted, or induced earlier in a less serious form, is a more open question. The state of the world economy, though it created problems outside the range of experience of businessmen and politicians, most of whom had never experienced conditions of serious economic recession, cannot be held to absolve either borrowers or lenders. Debtor countries, notably Mexico and Brazil, were pursuing unsustainable rates of economic expansion. The flight of domestic capital (discussed in Chapter 5), from Mexico,

Venezuela and Argentina especially, showed confidence falling at home long before it was lost abroad. When the lenders lost confidence they seemed to do so not only in response to individual country situations, but in relation to the developing country market as a whole. There was an element of contagion, even though it spread in only an attenuated form to the Far East.

With respect to Latin America, there has always been a tendency among investors to regard the region as a whole, not to differentiate sufficiently between the republics and to ascribe to them general characteristics so that they share a collective as well as an individual reputation in the markets. Nevertheless, the Latin American republics did have a common weakness that made them throughout the postwar period susceptible to balance-of-payments difficulties – namely, a pattern of economic growth that was internally driven rather than export-oriented, unlike the export-led economies of the Far East. The collective view was even more generally held in relation to Eastern Europe, for which the 'umbrella theory' was widely accepted by bankers: COMECON credit was held to be indivisible, and the USSR, with its vast resources and relatively small external debt, was believed to be unlikely to allow any of the organization's members to default, since that would impair the external financial relations of the whole bloc, including those of the USSR itself. In the event, the Polish and Romanian failures did have repercussions throughout the area, though least of all on the USSR.

Some such theory was in fact needed by lenders to Eastern Europe, for the criteria by which a country's creditworthiness might be judged could only to a very limited degree be applied to COMECON. Of its members, only Romania was then in the IMF, and only a few selected figures relating to the external sector of their economies were published; the level of international reserves was normally regarded as a state secret. For most countries the only way to analyse their balance of payments was through the trade statistics of partner countries in the West and the asset and liability positions vis-à-vis Western banks as reported through the BIS; other elements in the hard-currency position of COMECON countries were largely a matter of conjecture. While such analysis as was possible was not often very reassuring, lenders set great store by the punctilious regard hitherto shown by COMECON countries in meeting their contractual obligations.[4]

With borrowing countries in other areas the position was much more transparent. The larger countries had well-established statistical services; trade statistics for most countries were reasonably up to date; and balance-of-payments data were published locally in some form and were reported by member countries to the IMF (among whose lesser-known but important activities has been to work with developing countries on the improvement of their data), which published them in standardized form. Figures on international reserves, which should have been one of the most useful short-term indicators, were often published with much delay, and analysts were perhaps at fault in not giving sufficient weight to the non-appearance of data. Information on external debt had been compiled for developing countries as early as 1956 by the World Bank, which, like the IMF, did much to improve local statistics, under its debtor reporting system for long-term public and publicly guaranteed debt. Information on capital flows to developing countries was compiled by the Development Assistance Committee (DAC) of the OECD under its creditor reporting system. As noted earlier, the BIS received increasingly detailed information from central banks, based on the periodic returns submitted to it by commercial banks under its jurisdiction, of external assets and liabilities of banks in the reporting area vis-à-vis individual countries, including undisbursed credit commitments, through quarterly reports and in semi-annual reports that gave a maturity analysis. (Only the USA and the UK published corresponding figures for their own banks, and even up to 1986 they remained the only countries to publish regularly details of their banks' cross-border exposure on a fully consolidated basis.)

There was thus available a substantial amount of statistical information on the borrowing countries, but it was deficient in both consistency and timeliness, and before it could play a useful part in assessing the creditworthiness of sovereign borrowers, it needed to be analysed and presented in a form that was meaningful to the decision-makers. Analysis *ex post* of the deteriorating external financial position of borrowing countries that subsequently had to reschedule shows clearly how badly the situation was evolving from the 1980s onwards (though much less clearly up to 1979), and how dangerously high such key indicators as the ratios of interest service and total debt service to exports had become. At the time, the seriousness of the situation was not, it seems, so readily apparent, nor was it used to rein in banks' country exposure limits that lending officers, with their narrower horizons, had every incentive to use as fully as they were able. All statistics are published with delay: complete balance-of-payments figures could be a year in arrears; the World Bank's *Debt Tables* up to eighteen months, and covering private debt only partly, and no debt of less than one year's original maturity. Short-term debt could be calculated from BIS figures, but even those appeared some five to six months after the date to which they referred. Continuous efforts to improve the coverage, and where possible the timeliness, of international statistics were of course being made, and in many respects they have notably improved over the past four years.

The larger banks were certainly aware of the problems. As well as refining their internal systems for recording and monitoring their lending exposure, generated by operations conducted by perhaps hundreds of offices, they built up their capacity for economic analysis. As bank regulators and auditors took an increasingly close interest in the banks' systems of credit assessment, these were greatly strengthened. Indeed, a substantial literature on the subject of country risk assessment appeared from the later 1970s onwards, as well as specialized newsletters which provided, at a cost, their own credit-rating analyses and country commentaries. To establish appropriate limits for exposure to borrowing countries – which would include not only the major economies, both developed and developing, but many of the smaller states to which perhaps only trade-financing facilities were made available – the banks had not only to analyse, by means of their economic research departments, the latest data but to take a view on probable short- and medium-term economic and political developments. To choose a set of key economic indicators was not difficult, and these seem to be fairly standard among banks, but to devise an appropriate weighting system, and to incorporate factors that were not readily amenable to quantification, was a much more intractable problem. The techniques for the analysis of company accounts and domestic economic sectors are much longer established than those for the analysis of country creditworthiness, but this has not prevented lenders from suffering losses with loans to corporations and industries that, at least so far in the present decade, well exceed those incurred in sovereign lending.[5]

It remains arguable whether the large international banks could and should have better analysed the deteriorating position of the major developing country debtors and not have allowed their exposure to these countries to rise to the levels in relation to both capital and total assets that they did. Most banks would probably agree that their lending limits were set too high. The smaller banks, with only one or two economists, if any, on their staff, had to take much on trust. Managers of syndicated loans did, as noted earlier, make clear to participants that they were responsible for their own lending decisions, but it is not surprising that the smaller banks lost their appetite for foreign lending. The need to keep the smaller banks, especially the US regionals, in the picture was one of the reasons for setting up the Institute of International Finance (IIF), whose creation was agreed in principle at a meeting of senior bankers that took place at Ditchley Park, England, in the same month that the Mexican crisis broke.

Finally, in looking at the question of foresight on the part of lenders, it may be noted that it was the market that eventually gave the warning signals, not its regulators. The non-commercial financial institutions do not seem to have been much more perceptive: the IMF, which was incomparably in the best position to monitor current developments but whose reports were not made available to commercial banks, the World Bank and central banks. These institutions, though warning in general terms of the dangers of an excessive build-up of debt or analysing the problems of particular countries, did not, any more than the banks, anticipate the gravity of the crisis that was to occur in the second half of 1982. As a recent IMF commentary notes, 'it is clear in retrospect that there were shortcomings in the risk assessments made by private creditors and bank supervisors. At the same time, while Fund surveillance resulted in the transmission of warning signals to certain debtor countries in the context of Article IV consultations, it did not produce the perception of a global debt problem until a relatively late stage.'[6]

The circumstances leading to the build-up of the developing country debt crisis were unique in banking history. In retrospect it is hard to acquit the various parties – lenders, borrowers and the guardians of the system – of lack of foresight. But it must be remembered that the shocks to the international financial system, coming after a quarter of a century of unparalleled and virtually uninterrupted growth in the world economy, both developed and developing, found participants unprepared, in terms of experience and psychology, for economic recession and its consequences. The circumstances are hardly likely to recur: the lesson is no doubt the more general one that rapid changes in financial markets and techniques require a high degree of awareness and self-discipline among participants and of anticipation of problems by the regulators.

3

THE RESCHEDULING PROCESS

Whatever was lacking in anticipation, the reaction of the international financial community to the Mexican crisis was prompt. Within days of the announcement of the moratorium, and indeed before it came officially into effect, bridging loans totalling US$1.85bn, equally from the BIS and the US government, were mobilized, together with further official US facilities of US$1bn each for pre-payment of imports of Mexican oil and for commodity imports from the USA. The BIS, though properly insisting that it had no role as supplier of medium-term finance, even if it had sometimes had to renew bridging loans, played an indispensible role in several of the crisis situations of 1982–4, notably by providing liquidity to Hungary in 1982–3 – at that most difficult time before Hungary had joined the IMF or put into effect the internal reform measures that enabled it, if only temporarlily, to restore the balance in its external accounts.

The essential aim of rescheduling was to re-establish debt-servicing on a mutually agreed basis: for the creditor banks, to preserve the value of their loans; for the debtors, to reduce the annual cost of debt-servicing to their capacity to pay, giving due weight to their need to maintain an adequate level of imports. For both parties, the aim was to overcome an immediate crisis, to maintain conventional trading and financial links, and to encourage an early reactivation of spontaneous capital inflows. While in the last respect hopes were to be disappointed, the achievements of the initial rescheduling period from 1982 to 1985 should not be minimized, or the difficulties with which the negotiating parties on the whole successfully contended.

Liquidity could be provided in an emergency, but negotiation of a rescheduling agreement was a tortuous process. The Mexican rescheduling and associated 'new money' facility took about seven months to negotiate, but was not formally signed until almost exactly a year after the crisis broke. In the case of Argentina, a seemingly endless series of financial expedients and partly fulfilled arrangements, involving the IMF, the banks and other parties, dragged on into 1986.

Each country's debt situation had its peculiarities – Nigeria, for example, with its predominantly trade-related debt – but the approach to the problem of bank debt-rescheduling took a fairly standard form, building on experience with the Polish debt and other early cases.* The country requesting rescheduling would approach a number of leading creditor banks to form an advisory committee. The formal responsibility of the committee was thus to the debtor, which in turn was in principle responsible for the costs of the operation. The committee was not mandated by all the creditor banks to negotiate on their behalf; it discussed proposals and counter-proposals with the debtor country's team – usually central bank and ministry of finance officials, with perhaps a government minister present at the more important sessions. The largest creditor bank generally provided the chairman; other large lenders were also represented on the committee, which normally consisted of about a dozen members; a reasonably balanced country composition of the committee was desirable both for ease of communication with creditor banks and to ensure that differences in country attitudes were resolved at an early stage. For the UK the clearing bank with the largest exposure would normally represent the UK banks generally and communicate with them, and perhaps banks in some other European countries as well.

Even if the views of the leading banks on the committees carried a certain weight, they still had to persuade all the banks in the areas that they represented that the agreement reached in principle was sound and workable, and this could be especially difficult when 'new money' was required. If the banks on the advisory committee did not

---

* The larger the economy of the debtor country, the more complex the problems tended to be and the greater the skills and confidence of the negotiators who bargained on its behalf.

consult the other banks at each stage of the negotiations, they took good care to keep them informed, and in some cases a series of presentations were made to local banks at various centres around the world and regionally in North America. This was a lengthy process, and documentation and arranging signature by all creditor banks took longer still. Over 1,000 banks were said originally to have had claims on Mexico, but there was much double-counting due to banks' lending out of branches and subsidiaries in different financial centres. Nevertheless the totals were of the order of 600–700 for both Brazil and Mexico, and 400 even for a rather small country like Ecuador, though less than 50 for a few of the African states such as Togo and Zambia.

As well as negotiating the terms of rescheduling, the committees had many other laborious tasks to oversee, generally delegating them to a sub-committee. These included reconciliation of debt data from either side (one rescheduling operation is said to have covered 20,000 bank claims), establishing criteria for eligibility or exclusion, and ensuring the maintenance of short-term credit facilities. These last were not normally rescheduled, but repaid as they fell due, on the understanding that they would be renewed. In other respects, the net was cast as wide as possible, on the principle of equality of treatment; only secured loans such as ship mortgages were generally excluded (and of course export credits guaranteed by governments, which were rescheduled separately through the 'Paris Club'); co-financings with World Bank loans were included in early reschedulings, though the position now seems less clear-cut. A controversial area was and is the treatment of debtor country bonds and similar instruments held by creditor banks. Economic sub-committees, consisting of a small number of economists nominated by leading banks on the main committee, were also set up to evaluate the macroeconomic projections put forward by the debtors and to examine the cash-flow implications of proposed rescheduling terms.

Inevitably, the large US money-centre banks played a leading, in some cases even a dominant, part in these committees. In the Mexican Advisory Committee, US banks provided the chairman and six other members, with one member each from banks in the UK, Japan, Canada, West Germany, France and Switzerland. US banks made up at least half of the membership of the advisory committees for other Latin American rescheduling countries, with a few exceptions such as Panama and Cuba – where they were not, for obvious reasons, represented at all. In most cases US banks also provided the committee chairmen for western hemisphere countries, though sometimes with a European co-chairman or deputy, as they did elsewhere for Yugoslavia and Romania in Europe, for the Philippines (with a Japanese co-chairman) and for Liberia, Madagascar, Malawi, Senegal and Zambia. In the West Indies, Canadian banks led the committees for the Dominican Republic and Jamaica. UK banks provided the chairman, co-chairman or deputy for Ecuador, Honduras, Venezuela, Brazil and Malawi. A German bank headed the Polish committee, and French banks the committees for Cuba, Togo, Morocco and the Ivory Coast, the last two with US co-chairmen.

The key positions held by US banks in so many committees reflected their position as major lenders, especially in Latin America, though typically the exposure of US banks was more like one-third than one-half of the total. They also reflected the larger number of banks that US members of committees had to keep informed. But there were further reasons why the US interest in reschedulings often seemed paramount. US banks were subject to more strictly defined rules than banks in most other countries about the quality of certain assets in their loan portfolios, especially loans on which interest had fallen into arrears; they also produced quarterly profit-and-loss statements to which the market could be expected to react if there were a substantial increase in 'non-performing' loans.[7] For these reasons, the US banks were often prepared to go to great lengths to enable borrowers to keep interest payments current – as, for example, with the short-term loan provided by bank members of the advisory committee, plus four Latin American central banks (three of them in countries that were themselves rescheduling), in March 1984 to enable interest arrears in Argentina to be brought up to date at the end of the previous December. In the protracted negotiations with Venezuela, the slow process of registration of private-sector debt – a prerequisite for the authorization of service payments – appeared to cause more immediate concern to US banks than the terms of rescheduling of the much larger official debt.

Although there remained differences in attitude between US banks and those from other countries, there appears to have developed a notable degree of harmony in the advisory committees –

certainly in comparison with the Polish case, where national differences were very strong. The many rescheduling operations from 1982 onwards were treated as separate problems, though the same individuals often served on several committees and rescheduling became for some senior officials a full-time occupation. Each debtor country's situation had its peculiarities; there was no mechanism for considering them collectively, or any wish to create one. The banks followed the IMF in insisting that the case-by-case approach was the only practicable one; but precedents could be established, and concessions made to one debtor would inevitably be claimed by others in later negotiations. Hence the banks resisted from the beginning suggestions by debtors of interest-rate ceilings, capitalization of interest, and constant repayment schedules.[8] Interest-rate margins on rescheduled debt, periods of grace and the terms for repayment of principal could be negotiated and precedents created, but the amount of new money to be provided by the banks was necessarily a matter for case-by-case assessment.

When a debtor country declared a moratorium on capital repayments of medium-term debt, and even if it still kept interest payments up to date, banks naturally ceased new voluntary lending; it was as much as could be expected for them to keep open short-term credit lines. The essence of a rescheduling exercise was therefore to stretch out the period of capital repayments due in the years covered by the negotiations (initially only one or two), and since debtors were almost all running current-account deficits, they needed some balance-of-payments financing, of which part would be the banks' new money, during the period necessary to adjust their economies. One point on which the banks were adamant was that no new money could be provided unless the debtor country had in place an agreement with the IMF, with economic policy targets set out in a Letter of Intent as a condition for granting a Fund stand-by credit. Disbursements under the banks' new money facility, like those of the IMF, would depend on economic performance. This was the only way in which the banks could impose conditionality on sovereign borrowers. Experience with Peru in 1978 (at a time when that country refused to approach the IMF), and subsequently with Poland (not a member of the Fund until 1986), showed that the banks themselves could exercise little or no leverage to enforce compliance with specific economic policy targets in debtor countries.

Debt restructuring thus became a 'package deal' in which not only the banks and the IMF, but also the World Bank, US government agencies (for western hemisphere countries especially) and other parties, might be involved as providers of finance or because their interests were indirectly affected. A central role had to be taken by the IMF because the policy targets that it agreed with the borrower were linked to its estimate of the country's financing needs over the period – eighteen months or so – covered by the agreement. The banks were not necessarily pleased with the way in which this worked in practice, for it left them as residual suppliers of funds: i.e. what was still required after the IMF had totalled its own contribution, the likely amounts to be disbursed by the multilateral agencies, under bilateral export credits and from other official sources such as US commodity credits, and through any private inflows such as direct investment. This is what happened in the first Mexican rescheduling, when the residual financing requirement amounted to 7 per cent of existing bank exposure, and the IMF made a contribution of this size from the banks a condition for implementing its own part of the package. The advisory committees had to get the agreement of all creditor banks to put up a share pro rata to existing exposure; a certain amount of pressure was exerted on smaller banks that might have preferred to opt out of the arrangement, and resistance to such arrangements increased with time.

A new problem arose in the case of Venezuela when, in 1983, it requested a creditor-bank meeting to discuss rescheduling of official debt but made no request for new money: reserves and prospective current income, it claimed, would allow it to meet interest payments and all that it required was a stretching-out of bunched maturities. The banks made great efforts to persuade two successive Venezuelan governments – there was a hiatus in negotiations when agreement could not be reached before the elections in late 1983 and the new government did not take office until the following February – that an IMF programme was desirable. But the new government was as adamant as the old in insisting that the country's own adjustment programme was adequate. The banks eventually conceded the point and professed themselves content with 'enhanced surveillance' – meaning more frequent reviews of the Venezuelan economy of the kind that the Fund carries out under Article IV on all member countries.* Agreement in principle was not reached until September

---

* A form of monitoring applied later in the cases of Yugoslavia and Colombia.

1984, by which time the agreement had become a MYRA (see later), and various problems delayed the signature of the definitive agreement until early 1986. By this time, with the fall in the price of oil, Venezuela was again looking for a modification of its terms.

The Institute of International Finance
The need to keep all lending banks in the rescheduling process was one consideration in the establishment – on the initiative of a group of leading European, US and Japanese bankers – of the Institute of International Finance (IIF). Formally constituted in January 1983, it became operational about a year later. Its functions were carefully spelled out to make clear that it existed to provide information to its members on matters relating to international lending and to create a forum for discussion of current issues; in no way did it intend to function as a credit-rating agency or to influence the credit-related decisions of its members. Its founders were wary of US anti-trust legislation, and the IIF was not a collective spokesman for the commercial banks. Financial contributions to the Institute were determined pro rata to the size of each member bank's lending exposure to developing countries, so that the smaller banks were required to pay only a very modest annual sum. Its founder members comprised the leading US money-centre banks, the four major clearing banks in the UK and leading banks – except for one of the principal German banks – in Europe, and others from Japan, Canada and Brazil.[9] Membership was originally confined to banks that had direct exposure on borrowing countries, thus excluding investment and merchant banks, and other financial intermediaries that might have an indirect interest; but this condition was later relaxed. At mid-1986, the IIF had some 200 members, of which about 180 were banks. The Institute, which is located in Washington, acquired as its first managing director André de Lattre, a distinguished French banker who had latterly been working with the World Bank group.

The IIF, operating with a small but experienced staff, including personnel seconded by member banks and other financial institutions, has created an informational data base that is accessible to members 'on line', and produces – strictly for members – country analyses and reports, and sends its own economic fact-finding missions to market-borrowing countries. It has addressed itself, through study groups that include senior bankers from its membership, to various policy issues affecting banks as international lenders. Its informational services are highly valued by members, and no doubt especially so by the smaller banks that have little capacity for independent economic research. Save in its educational aspects, its role in relation to the debt question is not sharply defined; so far it has had no direct role in the rescheduling process, where the advisory committees appoint their own economic subcommittees (which doubtless benefit from the work of the Institute). A frequent if otiose comment has been that it might with advantage have been established four years earlier. Even so, it can still play a significant role in reinforcing the banks' own efforts to anticipate fresh problems in sovereign lending and – what may perhaps be of greater importance at the present time – alert them to improvements in debtor countries that might encourage a return to spontaneous lending.

Coincidentally with the creation of the IIF, in which leading Japanese banks participated, the Japanese government set up its own institute, the Japanese Centre for International Finance (JCIF), with a membership not only of banks, but of other institutions interested in questions of credit risk and issues related to the internationalization of financial markets.

Private-sector debt

When debtor governments approached the banks to discuss rescheduling, they were primarily concerned with the debts of the government itself or those it had guaranteed. The question of debts owed by the private sector soon arose, since governments had normally to provide the foreign exchange needed to service such debts, while creditor banks were concerned about their repayment in times of great economic stringency. If remittances were allowed through a controlled exchange market at preferential rates, the conditions had to be strictly defined; if through a genuinely free exchange market, the cost of continuing to service foreign debt might have brought borrowers to bankruptcy, because of the steep decline of most rescheduling countries' currencies. The problem was important only in those countries with a substantial private sector that had corporations large enough to enjoy access to foreign currency financing: in Mexico the private-sector debt was about US$15bn and in Venezuela US$7bn-8bn. Among these countries, the situation differed considerably. In Brazil, private-sector borrowing had largely been channelled through banks which on-lent to their local customers under prevailing regulations and whose obligations were included in official debt rescheduling.[10] In general, central banks agreed to provide private borrowers with foreign currency, with some guarantee against exchange risk, but sought the agreement of creditor banks to stretch out repayments over an agreed period – which the banks often thought too long in relation to the original maturity of the loans, especially since they themselves continued to bear the commercial risk.

The simplest solution (and of course the most convenient for creditors and debtors) was for the central bank to take over private-sector debts and to make its own arrangements for reimbursement in local currency, depending on the financial strength of the borrower; this was the case in Ecuador. Elsewhere, the position was more complicated. In Venezuela, the registration of private-sector debts was a slow process, as the government had to set up the necessary exchange-control department (Recadi), which investigated each private obligation, whether corporate or individual, to establish *bona fides* before registering it as eligible for servicing at one of the privileged exchange rates. Understandably, the government did not wish to subsidize operations related to capital flight. (Subsequently, in 1986, when oil prices had fallen, the government sought fresh arrangements, involving prolonged discussions with creditors, to stretch out repayment of these debts.) The system adopted in Mexico for making foreign currency available to private debtors (Ficorca) was of the type whereby foreign exchange was made available at a subsidized rate, but only if the debt was repaid over a number of years, with a period of grace. The commercial risk remained, and in 1985–6 foreign banks found themselves involved in financial restructuring arrangements for certain major corporations.

In some countries, governments have offered to consolidate various classes of private-sector debt into public bonds, but the term and yield on these do not seem to have been immediately attractive to creditors. In general, the question of private-sector debt, when not taken over by governments, has remained a difficult one, and the

31

position of trade creditors, with no recognized forum for collective negotiation, is even less satisfactory.

MYRAs

The rescheduling process moved into a new stage in 1984 with the negotiation of multi-year rescheduling agreements (MYRAs), of which that between the commercial banks and Mexico was the first to be concluded. The advantages were clear to both sides. Most countries had debt profiles requiring heavy repayments in the later 1980s; these would include some debt already rescheduled, since grace periods did not exceed four years and were sometimes shorter. The prospect of an annual series of negotiations, with all the organizational effort and use of executive time involved, was dismaying. The banks made a substantial concession in stretching out capital repayment periods to as much as fourteen years – later to twenty years – but this did at least make repayment look plausible. Other concessions were made on interest rates, so that the average margin over LIBOR to be paid by Mexico was 1.11 per cent on a rescheduled debt (which included debt already covered by earlier arrangements, as well as the new money) and as low as 0.875 per cent in 1985–6. The option of a margin over the more expensive US prime rate was dropped, as was the additional 1 per cent fee that had previously been normal in rescheduling. In all, US$48.7bn out of Mexico's total bank debt of US$72bn was covered by the agreement. Other MYRAs were negotiated for Venezuela, Yugoslavia and Chile among the larger debtors, and Ecuador, Uruguay, Jamaica and the Dominican Republic among the smaller. The move to multi-year rescheduling for the better-managed debtor countries was positively encouraged by the IMF and central banks, and by leading governments at the London summit meeting in June 1984, when the extension of the principle to official debts was admitted. In the event, the Paris Club achieved its first MYRA for official debts in 1985, for Ecuador.

Between 1983 and 1985 rescheduling of debt owed by 31 countries, totalling about US$140bn was negotiated by the commercial banks. In the same period the Paris Club rescheduled, for 32 countries – not necessarily the same ones – US$32.5bn of principal and interest owing in respect of guaranteed export credits. In support of the adjustment effort, the IMF had made available some

US$34bn to 72 indebted countries. An unprecedented degree of cooperation had been achieved between banks themselves and other participants on the lending side. Though bargaining had been hard, it could be said that creditors and debtors had maintained a sense of common interest: no debts had been repudiated and no country declared in default.

By 1984, when the economic recovery that had begun in the OECD countries in the previous year was continuing to strengthen, a certain degree of optimism about the debt situation had begun to emerge in the industrial countries, which was reflected in the IMF/ World Bank meetings of that year. The banks had been obliged to provide substantial amounts of new money in the form of 'involuntary' or 'concerted' lending: the justification of this – as it was the convention of public utterances on the subject to emphasize – was that the debtor countries had embarked on a painful but probably fairly short period of adjustment, and that when their external payments position was brought nearer to balance, they would regain access to the financial markets, and voluntary lending would be resumed. It was generally supposed that Mexico – which under its new government had made exemplary progress in meeting targets under the three-year agreement with the IMF – would continue to point the way. Brazil was seen as being at an earlier stage but moving in the right direction; Argentina had at least come to an agreement with the Fund; and Venezuela's problem was seen as one of liquidity rather than solvency. The situation in smaller debtors like Ecuador and Uruguay was improving, while in Eastern Europe hard-currency deficits were being brought under control or eliminated.

4
THE ADJUSTMENT PROCESS

The IMF approach and the reaction to austerity
If towards the end of 1984 there was some reason to expect that the debt problem was becoming manageable, developments in the following year were in many respects disquieting. The counterpart of the financial restructuring package was the acceptance by the debtor countries of an economic adjustment programme – usually agreed with the IMF, but sometimes self-imposed, as in Venezuela and Eastern Europe. Economic prescriptions related primarily to fiscal and monetary policy – areas which provided the quantitative targets that were easiest to monitor and which were central to the IMF's view that excessive monetary demand was the root cause of both inflation and external payments imbalances. Allied to this was an insistence on the restoration of effective price mechanisms in the foreign-exchange market, above all, and in interest-rate policy, public-sector pricing and the elimination of consumer subsidies, and a correspondingly lower reliance on quantitative controls on foreign trade and the allocation of credit. The IMF rightly denied that it sought deflation and a general recession of economic activity; it aimed at adjustment, of short duration, that would lay the foundation for renewed growth, and was disinclined to believe that there could be any alternative strategy.

In practice the adjustment involved heavier sacrifices on the part of debtors than had been foreseen, and their task was not much eased by developments in the world economy. Economic growth in the industrial countries slackened from 4.7 per cent in 1984 to 3.3 per cent in the following year. Interest rates had fallen from an average of nearly 17 per cent (LIBOR) in 1981 to about $8\frac{1}{2}$ per cent in 1985 and remained on a falling trend; but for countries borrowing at market rates this level still represented a severe burden, especially in conjunction with the evolution of their own terms of trade. The export prices of the fifteen heavily indebted countries (those listed on page 2 and again in Table 3) fell by 3.8 per cent in 1985, after a very slight recovery in 1984 that had itself followed a cumulative fall of 13 per cent in 1982–3, and continued to fall in 1986. Despite a fall in average import prices, the terms of trade of this group of countries worsened by 3 per cent in 1985, while the volume of their exports fell slightly, against a 9 per cent rise in 1984. Although the foreign trade performance of individual countries among the fifteen differed, their experiences in 1985 were broadly similar.[11] In 1986 the abrupt fall in petroleum prices was of course to alter the situation radically, and proportionately to have a greater impact on the balance of payments of the oil exporters than on that of the oil importers.

In these circumstances, balance-of-payments adjustment required a sharp contraction of imports, not too difficult in a few countries like Venezuela where manufactured consumer goods had figured largely, but much more so where industrial inputs were involved. The imports of the fifteen heavily indebted countries fell from US$133bn in 1981 to US$80bn in 1984. The trade balance swung from a deficit of US$5.5bn to a surplus of US$43bn over the same period, and the current account from a deficit of US$50bn to approximate balance. In 1984 and 1985 interest payments (including dividends) were of the same order of magnitude as the trade surplus (see Table 3). In contrast, developing countries without debt-servicing problems not only had a rather superior export per-formance, but were able to maintain or slightly increase imports and, in 1984, to finance a collective current-account deficit of US$14bn.

Such a turn-round in the balance of payments of the heavily indebted countries was not possible without a seriously depressive effect on economic activity. Real GDP in the group of fifteen fell in both 1982 and 1983, and the increase of just over 2 per cent in 1984 was insufficient to permit a rise in per capita GDP, which had suffered a cumulative fall of about 10 per cent since the beginning of the decade; a one per cent rise in 1985 in per capita incomes seems likely to be offset in 1986. If one excludes Brazil, which achieved $4\frac{1}{2}$

Table 3 Heavily indebted countries:* economic performance, 1981–6

	1981	1982	1983	1984	1985	1986†
(a) Trade and balance of payments (US$ bn)						
Exports f.o.b.	127.3	112.5	111.3	123.3	118 3	112.1
Imports f.o.b.	132.7	107.8	82.3	79.8	76.7	80.7
Trade balance	−5.3	4.7	29.0	43.4	41.4	31.1
Interest payments (incl. dividends)	−37.1	−44.4	−41.0	−45.7	−43.4	−39.1
Current-account balance	−50.1	−50.1	−13.8	−0.9	−0.1	−7.3
(b) Output (annual change, %)						
Real GDP	0.7	−0.4	−3.5	2.2	3.1	1.5
Real GDP per capita	−1.5	−2.8	−5.6	−0.2	1.0	−0.7

Source: Based on tables in IMF, *World Economic Outlook*, April 1986.
* Argentina, Bolivia, Brazil, Chile, Colombia, Ivory Coast, Ecuador, Mexico, Morocco, Nigeria, Peru, Philippines, Uruguay, Venezuela and Yugoslavia.
† Forecast.

per cent growth in 1984 and nearly 8 per cent in 1985, the picture is even less satisfactory.

The need to pursue policies of adjustment and austerity, with no clear prospect of that restoration of creditworthiness and resumption of economic growth which was the declared purpose of the exercise, inevitably produced a reaction. This was especially so in Latin America, where the largest number of problem debtors was concentrated. Many Latin American countries had had a considerable experience of working with the Fund, and attitudes towards that institution were ambivalent. There had grown up a school of economists that was deeply critical of the IMF and claimed that its prescriptions could not, because of structural rigidities in the Latin American economies, work as they did in developed countries. (Stabilization in Latin America had indeed often recorded partial or short-lived successes, but whether this was due to deficiencies in the prescriptions or failure to apply them wholeheartedly is by no means clear.)

Many politicians were influenced by the views of these economists, and many shared a way of thinking that was *dirigiste* by inclination and suspicious of unregulated free enterprise, whether domestic or foreign. Elsewhere, and sometimes in the same country by reaction, there were enthusiastic supporters of the market-oriented approach to economic management. In Latin America, as elsewhere, governments were at times glad of the existence of a body like the IMF to share some of the odium of restrictive economic policies; at other times, for domestic political reasons, they were reluctant to appear subservient to the Fund. They did not in any case necessarily accept that the IMF was the fount of all wisdom in economic matters, believing it to be excessively rigid in the choice of policy targets, and they escaped from its tutelage as soon as possible. Theoretical considerations were not of course paramount. The dangers of social discontent and political instability could not be ignored when real wages had fallen sharply and unemployment had risen, and politicians – in developing as in developed countries – were often willing to sacrifice medium-term policy to short-term expediency.

A few debtor countries never really attempted a Fund-related adjustment policy. In the case of Peru, agreements with the IMF in 1983 and 1984 either were suspended or did not become operative, nor had an effective agreement been reached by the end of 1986 with bank creditors, to whom interest payments were then well over two years overdue. The new government that took office in August 1985 unilaterally declared a ceiling of 10 per cent of export earnings for service of the medium- and long-term debt; it later fell into arrears with payments to the Fund itself and found itself increasingly isolated from the world financial community. Bolivia had suspended both principal and interest payments in March 1984, and there were virtually no developments in the debt situation for the next two years.

In Argentina nothing constructive could be done before the restoration of democracy and civilian rule in December 1983, and even then it was scarcely possible for the new government, had it wished to, to impose an economic programme that did not have growth and the raising of real wages as central themes. It was necessary for the economic situation to become patently dangerous before retrenchment could be accepted, and not until inflation reached an annual rate of nearly 1,000 per cent in mid-1985 did the government – with almost universal support – introduce its own stabilization scheme, the Plan Austral, that made possible a rapprochement on policy objectives with the IMF.

Elsewhere, Brazil had in 1985 ceased to give priority to IMF targets, even before the cabinet changes brought a new emphasis on economic expansion. Unlike most of the problem debtors, Brazil had responded early to changing circumstances by a vigorous policy of export expansion, in terms of commodities, manufactures and new markets. Diversification of trade made it easier for Brazil to adjust its external accounts after the debt crisis. With a trade surplus of US$12bn, it could for the time being service debt and needed neither the Fund nor new money from the banks. Mexico also fell short of its economic policy targets in 1985, even before the earthquake in Mexico City in September. The Minister of Finance and other spokesmen had frequently warned – even at the time of the signing of the MYRA – that although Mexico was willing to make every possible effort at adjustment, there were limits to what could be imposed.

The United Nations, and other international bodies in which the developing countries had a strong collective voice, constantly drew attention to the sacrifices being made by debtor countries and urged relief, though in general rather than specific terms. The establishment of the Cartagena Group of eleven Latin American countries, at a meeting in that city in June 1984, aroused some fear among creditors that a debtors' cartel might be in the making. On that occasion, and at subsequent meetings at Mar del Plata, Santo Domingo and Punta del Este over the next two years, various specific suggestions were made for debt relief; but differences in the economic situation of members of the group, and perhaps lack of political will, prevented declarations of principle being translated into a common programme of action. Nevertheless, the existence of the group served as a reminder to the creditor countries that the possibility of collective debtor action could not be excluded.

The Baker initiative

As 1985 progressed, it became increasingly apparent that a new initiative on the debt question was required, and this could only come from the USA. The political consequences of economic austerity, to which no term could be foreseen, and especially in neighbouring Latin American countries, was a matter of increasing concern in that country, which was also the base of the largest creditor banks. The so-called Baker Plan, named after the US

Secretary of the Treasury, was unveiled by him at the annual IMF/
World Bank meeting in Seoul in October 1985. Commonly referred
to as a plan, it is better called the Baker initiative, for it signalled a
new and more imaginative approach to the debt problem, rather
than offering a detailed plan of action. Nor did it in any way imply a
global solution: the case-by-case approach was firmly maintained.

The essence of the Baker initiative is that it takes a longer view of
the adjustment process and lays more stress on providing a foundation for economic growth. The IMF is envisaged as still having a
central role in respect to countries' short-term liquidity problems,
and just as the Fund's prescriptions are market-oriented in matters
of prices and exchange rates and trading policies, so are the
measures of structural reform foreseen in Baker. To assist in the
process, a greater role is assigned to the multilateral development
institutions, particularly the World Bank, which will continue to
expand its 'programme' lending in the form of structural and sector
adjustment loans, and the Inter-American Development Bank. A 50
per cent increase over previously projected levels for loan disbursements by the multilateral banks in the three years 1986–9, to fifteen
principal debtor countries, was foreseen; this would produce a gross
flow of around US$27bn over the period, and perhaps US$20bn net
of repayments. A further US$20bn in net lending by commercial
banks might also be forthcoming, if improved prospects for the
countries concerned provided the sort of new lending opportunities
that the banks could regard as commercially sound. The latter figure
implied an increase of $2\frac{1}{2}$ to 3 per cent annually in their exposure to
that group of countries. Further proposals in Baker – in which the
multilateral agencies rather than the banks would be involved – were
directed towards the needs of the poorest indebted countries, mainly
but not exclusively in Africa.

The fifteen Baker countries were those that the IMF classifies as
'heavily indebted'. Their collective debt to the banks at end-1985
was US$281bn, equal to about 60 per cent of the banks' exposure to
all developing countries, both OPEC and non-OPEC. Within this
group, five major Latin American debtors account for 80 per cent of
the total, and constitute the core of the debt problem as far as
commercial banks are concerned.

Of the total debt of this group of countries, amounting to some
US$444bn, 72 per cent is owed to the banks or other private
creditors; of the remainder, bilateral government lending (essentially

Table 4 Heavily indebted countries: total bank claims, end-1985 (US$ bn)

Argentina	28.9	Uruguay	2.0
Bolivia	0.6	Venezuela	25.8
Brazil	76.9	Ivory Coast	2.9
Chile	14.3	Morocco	4.8
Colombia	6.5	Nigeria	9.1
Ecuador	5.2	Philippines	13.4
Mexico	74.5	Yugoslavia	10.5
Peru	5.6		
		Total	281.0

Source: See Table 2 above, BIS Quarterly Report, October 1986.

guaranteed export credits) is the largest category at about 16 per cent of the total, with only about 7 per cent owed to the multilateral development agencies.

The reaction to the Baker initiative by leading OECD and debtor governments, the multilateral agencies and the banks was, with reservations, a positive one. The most unequivocal support came from the IMF and the World Bank. A Baker Initiative Committee of sixteen banks from leading financial centres was set up to consider its implications. Bankers' associations or other spokesmen in the USA, UK, Canada, Japan and – with some delay – the principal continental European countries issued statements or informed the IMF and the World Bank of their general support for the initiative. But continental European banks were notably more reserved than others, emphasizing the responsibility of governments in both creditor and debtor countries in providing the right climate for renewed bank lending. Several drew attention to the problem of capital flight, and some were inclined to query the list of countries, apparently finding it too closely aligned to US political and financial interests, a view for which the inclusion of one or two minor Latin American debtors may give some colour. In voicing collective support for the aims of the initiative, banks nowhere made a specific commitment to increase lending by any amount or to any individual or group of borrowing countries. As Baker's statement implied, their lending had still to be guided by their own commercial judgment. Banks in several countries also pointed out a notable gap in the initiative: the absence of any suggestion that governments should commit themselves to an increase in their own lending, whether in the form of aid or export-credit guarantees, let alone mention of even a tentative target for the next few years.

Finally, it should be noted that there was no intention in the Baker proposals that the fifteen nominated countries should benefit equally or proportionately, or that the list of countries was unchangeable. Responsiveness to structural reform measures would determine how quickly they became eligible. The scenario envisaged by Baker was that the implementation of adjustment policies by debtors, reinforced by better growth prospects, would lead to a restoration of creditworthiness and a return to spontaneous lending. That had indeed been the expectation behind the creditor countries' approach to the debt problem since 1982; it had not in fact been achieved by any rescheduling country, and whether it would do so now depended not only on developments in the debtor countries and on the effectiveness of the new strategy of official lending but, as far as the commercial banks themselves were concerned, on the priorities by which their lending policies would be guided. In the period since the debt crisis broke, the banks had perforce to re-examine the rationale of their cross-border lending policies, and that in a context of a rapidly evolving international financial environment. Their longer-term interests, and those of the debtor country governments, are considered in the following chapter.

5

CREDITOR AND DEBTOR INTERESTS

A. The banks

The commercial banks' fundamental interest is to compete in their chosen markets successfully and profitably, and to demonstrate to their depositors, shareholders and regulators that they can continue to do so. In this context, two basic questions presented themselves in the aftermath of the debt crisis: the propriety of continued cross-border lending to developing countries and the quality of their existing portfolios.

With the onset of the crisis in late 1982, new bank lending to developing countries fell sharply, and a large part was accounted for by 'involuntary' lending to rescheduling countries. Banks that had a large exposure to the problem countries were faced with a policy conflict: on one hand, their exposure to developing country borrowers collectively, and to major borrowers specifically, now seemed too high for prudence; on the other, they had to maintain the value of their portfolios, and this meant that they had to contribute through fresh lending, to the restoration or maintenance of debtor countries' solvency. The attempt to balance these two considerations runs through the whole banking attitude towards international lending since 1982 and seems likely to persist into an indefinite future. For smaller banks, whose exposure was lower in relation to their capital, the alternative of disengagement, and if necessary the writing off of existing loans, could be seen as a practical possibility that could be implemented over a fairly short time. For larger banks, whose exposure to problem countries was high in relation to capital, no such alternative course of action presented itself.

For this and other reasons, the philosophy of bank lending changed radically. No longer was asset growth in itself seen as a desirable objective; the quality of assets was more important, and business at low margins over the cost of funds, or better still fee-earning business 'off-balance-sheet', seemed far preferable to lending to developing countries, even at higher margins. This attitude affected lending not only to the problem countries, but to developing country borrowers generally. On the other hand, financial flows were being pulled strongly towards OECD countries and above all to the USA, which was increasingly in deficit with the rest of the world.

At the same time, far-reaching changes were taking place in the structure of both domestic and international financial markets. New financial instruments were being created, the roles of the different kinds of financial intermediary became less clearly defined and competition between these intermediaries was being intensified. These changes worked greatly to the advantage of prime borrowers, for whom the range of financing possibilities was widened and the cost cheapened, but were of little relevance to the needs of the indebted developing countries. Deregulation in various OECD countries was breaking down frontiers between markets and sectors of markets, and this gave banks a whole set of new preoccupations, both in their domestic and in their international affairs, and required them to evolve new strategies of business development in which the developing countries could be only marginally involved. It was not here a question of deliberate exclusion of developing country borrowers, but that the more sophisticated financial techniques being developed were directed towards preserving the banks' share of business with corporate customers in developed industrial countries, and these forms of financing were unlikely to be appropriate for borrowers in many developing countries.

The changes in the mainstream of financial flows after 1982 meant that funds were being recycled increasingly between surplus and deficit OECD countries, rather than from OPEC to developing countries. Accompanying this was a change in the preferred financial instrument: bond issues progressively displaced the syndicated bank credit that had been characteristic of the 1970s. In 1981 the total of syndicated loans arranged in the eurocurrency markets was US$132bn, and bond issues amounted to US$44bn; in 1985 the proportions were reversed, syndicated loans amounting to only US$21bn, while international bond issues rose to US$164bn.

The fall in interest rates after 1981 could in any case have been expected to lead to a revival in the bond markets, but the process of 'securitization' in lending (or disintermediation) has continued – for reasons that are directly related both to the changing pattern of world surpluses and deficits and to the developing country debt crisis itself. OPEC investors had preferred bank deposits to bonds; with industrial country investors, the preference went increasingly the other way. Industrial country borrowers were glad to have renewed access to bond financing at reasonable rates, but investors' appetite for the bonds of developing country borrowers remained small and highly selective. Another factor was that the debt crisis had not been without an effect on the banks' own standing in the market, so that investors often preferred to lend direct to the end-users of the funds, rather than through the intermediary of a bank deposit. For their part, the banks in most countries – Japan being the most notable exception – being less concerned with the growth of asset volume than with capital/asset ratios, were glad to expand their fee-earning, off-balance-sheet business by arranging security issues for their customers rather than lending the money themselves, though they could of course, if they wished, hold some part of the issue in their own portfolios.

As well as international bond issues in more or less traditional form, there has been a rapid expansion of the market for floating rate notes (FRNs), issues of which amounted to US$56bn in 1985. As floating rate instruments they are the nearest equivalent to the syndicated roll-over credit; the advantage for the banks, which have themselves invested heavily in them, is that they are marketable, while participations in syndicated credits are not – except through a relatively small and highly discounted market. Borrowers in a few developing countries have been able to issue FRNs – notably in the Far East, South Korea, Malaysia, Hong Kong and Thailand – and have used the proceeds to repay bank credits, or as a substitute for new bank borrowing. Disintermediation has also affected the short end of the borrowing market with the development of commercial paper markets and innovations such as note-issuance facilities; here, once more, there are few borrowers in developing countries that are eligible for these forms of financing, though South Korea is again one of the few exceptions. Other innovations have taken place in the interest-rate and exchange-rate futures markets. As a result of all these changes, the development of banking business and the priority considerations for bank boards and senior management are far removed from what they were in the 1970s.

Business with developing countries remains of course an important activity for commercial banks based in the major financial centres, and still contributes a significant, if generally declining, share of profits. Short-term trade finance is normally self-liquidating and remunerative; banks appear to have few reservations about increasing such facilities to developing countries with an expanding foreign trade and have generally maintained them for rescheduling countries. (Even when Peru fell into arrears with service of its medium-term debt, it continued to reimburse trade credits and to pay interest on them, and short-term debt was exempted from the ceiling placed on total debt-service payments. Creditor banks only gradually withdrew such trade facilities.) Another important connection with developing countries for the larger banks, especially in the USA and UK, is provided by their extensive branch networks, through which they carry out local currency financing for both domestic and international customers. Attitudes towards medium-term foreign currency lending, of the kind envisaged in the Baker initiative, remain, however, highly selective, although there are some difficulties in measuring the size of the net contribution that the banks are making to developing country finance.

Bank lending to developing countries must of course continue, at least to an extent that replaces maturing debt by new finance, if the borrowing countries are not to make a progressive repayment of capital. The need to make such repayments would in many cases precipitate a rescheduling, which would certainly not be in the interests of the banks. The package of loans totalling US$1bn agreed at the end of 1985 for the Colombian government, central bank and state energy corporations should no doubt be seen in this perspective, and possibly also the syndicated credit of US$350m on very favourable terms for Malaysia that was announced in August 1986. Not all lending should of course be seen as having a precautionary character: in 1985 there was a sharp increase in borrowing by East European countries, particularly the USSR and East Germany, but also Hungary and Bulgaria, as well as by some Asian countries, notably China (regarded as an especially attractive borrower), India

Table 5 Bank credit commitments to developing countries, 1979–85 (US$ bn)*

		1979	1980	1981	1982	1983	1984	1985†
Africa	A	4.8	2.6	4.1	2.7	2.7	0.5	1.0
	B	—	—	—	—	—	—	0.1
Asia	A	11.0	9.2	12.8	12.6	10.4	9.3	2.9
	B	—	—	—	—	—	0.9	—
Europe	A	7.8	4.9	4.7	3.7	2.9	3.4	2.3
	B	—	—	—	—	0.6	—	—
Middle East		0.2	0.7	0.2	0.6	0.7	0.4	—
W. hemisphere	A	26.0	20.4	25.2	23.0	2.0	0.6	0.2
	B	—	—	—	—	13.3	14.8	2.2
Total, capital-importing DCs	A	49.8	37.8	47.0	42.6	18.7	14.2	6.4
	B	—	—	—	—	13.9	15.7	2.3

Source: IMF, *International Capital Markets: Developments and Prospects*, Occasional Paper 43 (Washington, DC, February 1986), p.38.
* Publicly reported long-term external credits.　† First half.
A = spontaneous lending; B = concerted lending.

and South Korea. In the first half of 1986, the creditworthy OPEC borrowers returned to the market.

Overall, however, new bank credit commitments to developing countries that were publicly reported declined steadily from 1983 onwards: OECD figures show that borrowing in the first five months of 1986 by non-oil developing countries, at an annual rate of less than US$7bn, were the lowest for over a decade. Table 5 shows new bank long-term credit commitments, both 'spontaneous' and 'concerted', between 1979 and 1985. Reflecting market conditions, the spread on international bank loans fell steadily from 1983 to the first half of 1986, when borrowers in Eastern Europe were paying on average little more than a quarter of one per cent and less than the average of about 0.4 per cent paid by OECD borrowers, while non-OPEC developing country borrowers were paying, on spontaneous lending, an average of 0.7 per cent.[12] Seen against the background of the debt crisis, these lending margins may seem surprisingly small, but the market for developing country loans had of course become much smaller and more selective, while the low margin on East European borrowing may have been influenced by the fact that major borrowers were using the proceeds at least partly to restore liquidity.

A measure of the change in total *net* bank lending is given by the BIS consolidation of bank exposure data. Figures for 1983–5 relating to non-OPEC developing countries and to Eastern Europe are summarized in Table 6. The figures in the last two columns have been adjusted to take into account variations in the exchange rate of other lending currencies against the US dollar.

Table 6 Bank external claims, BIS-reporting area, 1983–5 (US$ bn)

	End 1983	End 1984	End 1985	Change 1984–5	Adjusted change 1984–5	% adj. change 1984–5
Latin America	208.8	212.3	218.0	+5.7	+1.6	+0.8
Middle East	16.2	15.4	16.5	+1.1	+0.2	+0.1
Africa	19.8	18.8	21.6	+2.8	+0.8	+0.4
Asia	80.0	84.5	95.8	+11.3	+8.2	+9.7
Total, non-OPEC DCs	325.7	331.0	351.9	+20.9	+10.8	+3.3
Eastern Europe	52.0	48.2	60.5	+12.3	+5.6	+11.6

Source: BIS Quarterly Reports (see Table 2).

These figures suggest a general unwillingness on the part of banks to acquire additional exposure on developing countries. Unadjusted figures for US and UK banks for the twelve months ended June 1985 showed an overall decline in their claims on developing countries: whereas all bank lending to capital-importing developing countries rose by 1.6 per cent in that period, that of US banks fell by 4.8 per cent and of UK banks by 2.0 per cent. Furthermore, there was an apparent decline in bank claims on even the more creditworthy areas and countries: reported claims on South Korea in this period rose by 7.5 per cent, while those of US and UK banks fell by 10.0 per cent and 7.9 per cent respectively. This may be in part at least a result of securitization, so that banks' holdings of instruments such as FRN had not been incorporated in the data for some countries. Other factors also produce changes in exposure data: lending may fall out of the statistics when loans are charged off or sold, when guarantees are called or as a result of a transfer of ownership. For these various reasons, the Federal Reserve has estimated that US banks' lending to non-OPEC developing countries may have been underestimated by about $3\frac{1}{2}$ per cent in 1983–4. Even so, total US bank lending to developing countries is still seen to be declining. That there was in fact a total recorded increase in bank exposure, especially in the Far East, must be largely if not entirely attributed to the growing international activity of Japanese banks, whose external assets were growing rapidly in 1984 and 1985, and especially their lending in yen. Data for the first half of 1986 confirm the trend and show an increase of only US$4.3bn in the dollar value of bank claims on non-OPEC developing countries; the exchange-rate-adjusted flow figure for the six months shows a decrease of US$4.7bn, but a positive flow of US$2.4bn to Eastern Europe.

To fulfil the role set for them in the Baker initiative would put the banks in a dilemma as to how their 'commercial judgment' should really guide them. All fifteen of the designated countries either have rescheduled, are due to reschedule, have restructured loans or are seriously in arrears. The dilemma is one that is shared by their regulators – the central banks or other supervisory authority. Banking prudence suggests that provisions should be made out of profits to cover the risk of loss on existing loans; the broader considerations underlying the Baker approach require that the flow of capital to the debtor developing countries should be maintained. An analogy may be drawn with corporate bank customers that find themselves unable to meet their commitments: unless the company is hopelessly insolvent, the banks will try to save it by restructuring the debt, quite likely by providing additional funds and at the same time making a thorough examination of the company's assets and liabilities, forming a view of its business prospects and if necessary insisting upon changes in its management and organization. In doing so, they protect the value of their loans and may hope for eventual repayment, instead of whatever partial recovery they might make by forcing the company into receivership. There is some parallel with a sovereign debtor, but there are important differences. The fact that a country cannot, like a bankrupt company, cease to exist provides little safeguard, since it can in the last resort repudiate its debts. Nor is the control of debtor policy exercised by the IMF or the World Bank as tight as that which can be exerted on a private company.

On the other hand, the risks to individual banks and to banking systems with sovereign lending are potentially much greater. To lend new money while at the same time making loan-loss provisions against existing loans to the same borrower is not as illogical as it may seem, providing that the new money – and the conditions on which it is supplied – improve the quality of the existing loans. With the additional funds, a 5 per cent provision might be deemed adequate, say, but without them perhaps 10 per cent would be more appropriate. Unfortunately, risk and the appropriate level of provisions cannot be measured with such accuracy. What can be said is that if the dual process is to be credible, it must show an improvement in the debtor's position within a reasonable period; rescue operations for a private company will not be repeated many times. Reschedulings and injection of new money in the form of concerted lending would likewise at some point cease to be credible, since, in the absence of an increasing level of provisions, the banks would be taking into profits the interest income on debt that had been made possible only by their fresh lending, and at the same time would be adding to assets whose worth was supported only as long as the process continued. Without suggesting that this point has been reached, it is at least unfortunate that the first substantial commitment of new funds since the Baker initiative was for a concerted package for Mexico, so that instead of moving into a new phase, where the additional exposure taken on by the banks would be spontaneous, it looks very much like a pre-Baker rescue operation, with the addition of longer-term money from the World Bank.

The question of an appropriate level of provisions is one on which banks and their regulators in different countries appear to have markedly divergent views. In some countries, notably the UK, the approach is pragmatic and not subject to formal rules; the banks set their own levels under the guidance of the Bank of England. In others, problem countries are listed by the supervisory authorities, and the percentage of the loans outstanding to those countries that must be covered by provisions is laid down for particular countries or collectively. This applies to sovereign debt; provisioning against private debt in developing countries naturally requires the commercial risk to be taken into account.

The rules on provisioning are not generally published in detail, but it seems that in centres where the authorities list countries for which provisions are required, levels are higher than where the approach is discretionary. Levels appear to be substantially higher in continental European countries than elsewhere: in Switzerland, from 10 to 50 per cent, with an average of about 20 per cent; in Sweden, up to 80 per cent; in the Netherlands, from 5 to 100 per cent; and also in West Germany. In all these countries, major bank provisions are thought to be in the 20 to 50 per cent range for problem debtor countries. Elsewhere, Canadian banks were required to set up by end-1986 reserves of 10 to 15 per cent for loans to 32 countries, while in Japan provisions must be made out of after-tax profits of up to 5 per cent on both new and existing loans to 33 countries. In the USA the discretionary approach applies generally to provisions, but, as noted earlier (Chapter 3, note 6), accounting regulations are strict, if not totally inflexible, in relation to loans on which interest is more than 90 or 180 days overdue. In the case of Peru, loans to which have been placed in the 'value-impaired' category, an initial provision of 15 per cent is understood to have been required. If, as is widely supposed, average provisions in the USA against loans to problem debtor countries is around 5 per cent, and for UK banks in the range of 5 to 10 per cent, then the three largest groups of lending banks, those based in the USA, the UK and Japan, have by far the lowest provision rates.[13]

An important consideration for banks is the tax treatment of provisioning, and this again is far from uniform as between countries. In the UK, provisions may be either specific (and attract tax-relief) or general (and not eligible to be set against tax). The principle that, if tax relief is given, the provision cannot be taken into capital accounts is general, and seems to apply in continental European countries, where tax relief is more generous. In the UK, major clearing banks reported in 1986 for the first time that they had made specific provisions against sovereign debt. Setting a reserve of any kind against a debt, or even writing off the loan, does not mean that it is forgiven or that claims against the borrower cannot be revived. The possible reaction on the part of individual sovereign states to the knowledge that creditor banks were making large provisions against their loans to them, provides one reason for keeping the rules on practice in these matters confidential.

The requirement to make provisions against loans to sovereign debtors, and especially where no tax allowances are granted, must colour the attitude of potential lenders to taking on additional exposure, whether voluntary or as a further exercise in concerted lending. The wide difference in practice between the major financial centres out of which the international banks operate suggests greater difficulties in the future in keeping creditors together when new money requirements are being negotiated and apportioned. Countries that now take a discretionary and 'bank-by-bank' approach to provisioning may move towards a more uniform system (there is reason to believe that the Bank of England may at least offer some guidelines on the subject), but it is difficult to see how the different systems in use could be brought into line. There is no system for evaluating country risk that does not involve a large measure of subjective judgment, and the levels at which mandatory provisions are fixed by bank regulators must be influenced by other considerations of policy and be related to the structure and strength of the national banking system. The Bank Supervisors Committee of the BIS has been studying comparative practice with regard to provisions, as it has questions of the measurement of capital and capital adequacy, but there is no reason to suppose that such studies will lead to any internationally agreed criteria in the foreseeable future. These questions are not of course related only to country risk but to risks arising from the banks' new involvement in security markets; again, the debt problem is not the only preoccupation.

Provisions, the rebuilding of capital and the improvement of capital/asset ratios are related, in that they all strengthen the balance-sheet. The relatively low level of general provisions against sovereign debt in the US is justified locally by the improvement that has taken place over the past five years in capital ratios. The onset of the developing country debt crisis came at a time when the capital/asset ratios of banks in many countries had been weakening for some years. Bearing in mind the decline in quality of lending to domestic borrowers in some sectors that had suffered particularly in the recession, central bank governors of the Group of Ten collectively agreed in 1982 that the erosion of banks' capital positions should be reversed, and this recommendation has been generally followed through.

Thus, in the USA, the three supervisory authorities – the Federal Deposit Insurance Corporation (FDIC), the Comptroller of the

Currency and the Federal Reserve Board – now impose similar requirements on the different classes of bank that they supervise. Since 1984–5 the largest banks have been required to increase primary capital to $5\frac{1}{2}$ per cent of assets, and total capital to 6 per cent. All banks have now moved above the minimum and no new minimum has been set. As a result of the rapid growth of capital and a slower rate of growth of assets, the US money-centre banks' capital/asset ratios improved from an average of 4.7 per cent in 1981 to 6.1 per cent in 1985; for a representative group of regional banks the increase was from 6.3 per cent to 7.2 per cent.[14] Nevertheless, exposure to leading debtor countries remained high, if declining, in relation to capital. For nine money-centre banks, exposure to the fifteen 'Baker initiative' countries at the end of June 1986 was the equivalent of 129 per cent of capital; to Brazil alone, 36 per cent; and to Mexico, 31 per cent. For individual banks, exposure to one of these largest debtor countries may be considerably higher.

Lack of comprehensive information makes it impossible to carry out a comparable analysis for other industrial countries' banks. Nevertheless, according to the IMF, 'for the industrial countries as a group, the bank capital ratio appears to have returned in 1984 to the 1977 level, although this was not the case for each country within the group'.[15] Given that a substantial part of the foreign assets of non-US banks is denominated in dollars, while capital is denominated in domestic currency, the ratio is significantly affected by changes in currency values, and the decline in the dollar since 1985 will have helped to build up the capital ratios of these banks. How far the rebuilding of capital, together with the gradual reduction in the proportion of total bank international claims accounted for by loans to developing countries, will be seen by banks in different countries as providing a basis for future growth in lending to these countries is by no means clear.

One area of potential problems is that the sources of new bank financing may become progressively more restricted to a relatively few larger banks in a smaller number of countries. As noted above, different policies on provisions and write-offs may make it more difficult to maintain unanimity among rescheduling groups; in this respect, the arrangement of the banks' contribution to Mexico's financing in late 1986 seemed likely to prove a test case. There is also a potential problem in that present exposures may be getting

increasingly out of line with those prevailing when the first reschedulings took place, not only because of write-offs but because of
swapping of exposures, which for one or two large US banks is
believed to have taken place on a fairly substantial scale.

More uncertain still is the continuing role of the smaller banks.
Although large banks in most countries may still continue to
recognize their common interest in sustaining the economies of
debtor countries, this is not necessarily the case for smaller banks,
especially in the USA, where they are numerous, but also in
Europe. If their exposure on a particular borrowing country is small
in both absolute terms and in relation to capital, they can gradually
write off their loans and perhaps recoup some of the loss by selling
them in the secondary market, even at a deep discount – an option
not open, for reasons of scale, to the larger banks. Although the
smaller banks collectively may hold only a rather low proportion of
a rescheduling country's debt, say 10 to 20 per cent, depending
where the line is drawn, to allow them to drop out of the process
would leave the remaining banks to make up the difference, and
encourage banks just above the minimum exposure level also to seek
exemption from putting up their share of new money. As the
problems of maintaining unanimity among the banks can only
become more difficult with time – or at least until some distant date
when existing loans are not significantly large items in the banks'
balance-sheets – this suggests that, after a limited number of
rescheduling operations for any borrower, some new method of
refinancing will be unavoidable.

B. The debtor governments

The heavily indebted countries have for the past four years been
making a substantial net transfer of resources back to the capital-
exporting countries. Their basic concern must be to reverse these
backward flows, which require them to run large export surpluses on
traded goods and services. To achieve these surpluses by increasing
exports is particularly difficult for countries still dependent on oil
and other commodities, and most of the problem debtors have had
to meet the situation by the more painful route of reducing imports,
domestic demand and output. While the expansion and diversification of exports has a central role in the strategy of the debtors, they
also look for more immediate ways of reducing these reverse

transfers, by minimizing the cost of debt service and attracting additional, and preferably non-debt-creating, flows.

Debt relief

The debtor countries' basic interest is to reduce as far as possible, if not eliminate, the burden of debt-servicing. This might be done by a refunding operation that went well beyond the terms of current rescheduling arrangements. Numerous suggestions have been made by academic and other commentators for a general, or collective, solution – in contrast to the case-by-case, country-by-country approach – to the debt problem. Ingenious and even plausible as some of these schemes are, they have never received any response from those parties on the creditor side who would have to implement and finance them. Any such response would require a concerted effort and a unanimity of approach on the part of OECD governments. The organizational problems would be considerable, and decisions on eligibility might involve making invidious distinctions: the problem debtors and the imprudent borrowers are not necessarily the poorest countries. Effective relief for major debtor countries would need to be financed – by governments out of budgetary revenue either directly or indirectly, by banks (which would take a loss through income forgone) or, if by third parties, then with some form of collective government guarantee. The global solution to the problem of developing country debt still looks far outside the realm of practical politics.[16]

A radical solution to the debt problem on the part of a debtor would be repudiation or the declaration of an indefinite moratorium on both capital and interest payments. If a net transfer of resources abroad was foreseen for an indefinite period by a calculation of the balance between the cost of continuing to service debt and prospective new borrowing forgone, then repudiation might seem in arithmetical terms advantageous. Explicit repudiation of debt has in fact been extremely uncommon, and has been confined to cases where revolution has established a communist regime that claims to make a complete break with the past and accepts no responsibility for the acts and commitments of the old regime. It is most unlikely that any other kind of government would wish to issue such a challenge to the capitalist world. Where revolutionary governments have taken power in recent decades – as in Iran and some African countries

– their disavowal of contracts entered into by the previous regime has been limited to specific transactions that they deem corrupt.

A declaration of an indefinite moratorium on bank debt, or failure over a long period to negotiate seriously with creditors on a resumption of debt service, is rather more easily conceivable. Apart from the morality of such action, and the effect that it would have on the country's standing in the world, the practical consequences would be incalculable. Assets abroad might be at risk; new loans from the multilateral agencies and other official sources would probably be unobtainable, even if debts to these institutions were still being correctly serviced. Commercial credit would either be unavailable or available only at a high cost, though fellow debtors would no doubt continue to trade on normal terms. Much trade might have to be conducted on a cash or barter basis. A considerable effort of internal economic adjustment would be required, and both politicians and administrators would face a host of unfamiliar problems. None of these problems might in the last resort be insuperable, especially for a country with a high degree of self-sufficiency. It is fair to add that no major debtor country has threatened such action, nor, with one possible exception, does it seem to have been seriously considered.

Debtor countries may nevertheless be expected to press continually for better terms on rescheduled debt, particularly on interest rates. An interest-rate 'cap' would defer interest payments above a ceiling rate until the rate had fallen below another indicated level or would postpone these payments by stretching out the loan. Constant repayment schedules are not of course unknown in domestic banking in some countries. The World Bank has also made at least one such loan – to Paraguay in 1984 – in a co-financing with commercial banks, in which the World Bank committed itself to repurchase any remaining portion of the loan still held by the banks after the original maturity of ten years. Limiting debt-service payments to a proportion of annual export earnings is also frequently urged, and has been unilaterally imposed by Peru. From Brazil has come a suggestion that debt service should be limited to a certain percentage of GDP. Proposals of this kind have always been unacceptable to the creditor banks. They may not be resistible for ever, but if interest paid falls below the cost of funds, or if ceilings are set on annual debt service, the banks cannot be expected also to find new money, whether in concerted or in spontaneous form.

Other capital inflows

Non-debt creating flows seem one of the most desirable ways of helping to close the prospective financing gap of the heavily indebted developing countries. Flows of these kinds – very largely, if not entirely, direct investment – have fallen off considerably since the debt crisis, from US$7.4bn to the 'Baker Fifteen' in 1982 to US$4.1bn in both 1984 and 1985. This no doubt reflects in part the recession in some countries, but it is also the case that creditworthiness tends to be indivisible, so that a country that cannot meet its contractual obligations on debt is likely to seem unattractive to equity investors as well.

On the debtor side, attitudes towards foreign direct investment have in many countries become much more accommodating; old prejudices have been set aside, if not abandoned, and regulations that hamper the entry of foreign investment into key sectors of the economy relaxed. Effort to improve the efficiency of the public sector is now generally recognized, even without the encouragement of the multilateral agencies, to require the disbandment or sale of many public-sector enterprises. Privatization has increased the opportunities for investment by foreign and domestic capital, including capital held abroad, and the conversion of debt into equity provides a means for such investment that is advantageous to both governments and investors. Provisions on debt/equity conversion were incorporated in the MYRAs for Chile and Mexico. Chile has proceeded furthest in implementing the idea, and has formalized the procedures whereby both foreigners and nationals, under separate arrangements for direct investment and for general purposes, may exchange debt denominated in foreign currency for pesos at its face value, which for holders who have purchased debt at a discount of perhaps 30 per cent or more gives a large incentive. In its first year of operation, the scheme covered conversions by residents totalling US$239m, and by foreigners US$128m. Elsewhere progress has been slower; but, in Mexico, Nissan of Japan made a US$50m investment via a debt conversion operation, and examples have been reported from other Latin American countries, including Brazil. An announcement by the Philippine government of its intention to set up its own scheme, with the cooperation of foreign banks, was made in August 1986. There is also scope in countries with reasonably developed securities markets for expansion of portfolio investment under schemes such as those sponsored by the International Finance Corporation (see Chapter 6).

As the legislation in Chile and other countries recognizes, domestic capital held abroad is a large potential source of balance-of-payments financing. Sympathy among bankers for the problem debtor countries has undoubtedly been weakened by the extent to which outward transfers of domestic capital took place during the years when the external debt was being built up. Various estimates of the amounts of flight capital have been made; they can only be approximate, and have been challenged by Mexico and other countries. They are derived essentially from recorded private capital movements in the balance-of-payments data, an assumption that residual negative balances can also be attributed to private capital, and apparent undervaluation of exports. Some private capital may of course be held abroad for perfectly legitimate reasons – to finance trade or provide working balances, or for normal portfolio diversification – but the scale of these apparent outward capital movements is such as to suggest a widespread and sustained distrust of domestic currencies and markets.

One estimate is that total outflows during the years 1976–85 amounted to US$26bn for Argentina, US$53bn for Mexico, US$30bn for Venezuela, and a relatively moderate US$10bn for Brazil.[17] These amounts are the equivalent of 90 per cent, 72 per cent, 115 per cent and 13 per cent, respectively, of the total bank debt of these countries outstanding at the end of 1985. A private estimate for the period 1979–85 gives a total outflow for Argentina, Brazil, Chile, Mexico and Venezuela of US$102bn, equal to 53 per cent of all debt accumulated during that period. If these magnitudes are approximately correct, the interest received on the investments they represent would – if remitted back to the countries of origin – cover more than half the current cost of debt-servicing. Where outflows have slowed down, more realistic exchange rates, more effective controls and tighter monetary policies have doubtless helped – as in Mexico, where a reflow of some US$3bn was estimated for the first quarter of 1986. Realistic exchange rates, competitive interest rates and adequate domestic investment outlets are all needed to provide a counter-attraction to investment abroad, but the general question of confidence in economic and political systems is no doubt of overriding importance. No massive reflux of flight capital can in any likely circumstances be envisaged, nor indeed could monetary systems cope with it, but at least to reverse the direction of net flows and to sustain an inward movement should be an important aim of debtor country policy.

6
OTHER PARTIES

A. The multilateral agencies

The IMF
Whatever the changes of approach to the debt problem, the IMF must continue to play the central role in the complex financial diplomacy that governs the relationships between debtor and creditor governments, the other multilateral institutions and the banks. In mid-1986, of the fifteen Baker countries, all but two had active 'stand-by' agreements with the Fund, were negotiating or renegotiating them, or were operating under 'enhanced surveillance' arrangements. The requirement, by the Paris Club and by the banks, of the IMF's 'seal of good housekeeping' in one form or another, as a condition of rescheduling, is not likely to be abandoned.

Of the two exceptions, Brazil has been able to dispense with new money from either the Fund or the banks because of its exceptionally strong foreign trade position, although whether this could be sustained beyond 1986 began to look increasingly doubtful. Peru is a difficult case, for, having fallen into arrears with payments to the IMF due under earlier arrangements, it has been declared ineligible for further assistance from the Fund until the position is regularized; this must also jeopardize its relations with the World Bank. Previous occasions on which the Fund has reluctantly declared ineligibility have been in relation to small debtors such as Guyana and some African states; Peru is the first major debtor in this position, and in view of its bad relations with the international banking community its position is becoming increasingly isolated. Dialogue with the IMF has not been completely broken off: consultation with all members at regular intervals is normal under the IMF's rules, and Peru has not suggested that it might withdraw from membership – which no country has done since 1959. The new and more flexible form of conditionality may eventually make a rapprochement possible; if not, then Peru will become in all respects a test case.

Not only has the IMF played the key role in the debt-rescheduling process; it might also be said that rescheduling and its attendant problems have become the central activity of the IMF. Over the past fifteen years there has been a substantial erosion of its responsibilities in respect to the industrial countries and their financial relationships. Its functions have become marginal in relation to the world exchange-rate system since flexible exchange rates have become general, and it has not made any loans to an OECD country since 1977. Developing countries might argue that the Fund's thinking and procedures did not evolve quickly enough to respond to their own changing needs, even though it did introduce new financing facilities and cautiously extend the term of its lending. Because of its concentration on the provision of short-term adjustment finance, there has been a marked reduction in its net disbursements to developing countries since the first rescheduling operations: against an outflow to these countries of US$11bn in 1983, a point was reached somewhere around mid-1986 when there was a net reflow back to the Fund. There was also an appreciable tightening of conditionality in the 1980s, justified perhaps in view of the magnitude of the adjustment required, but contrasting with the more relaxed attitude of the 1970s, when recycling and the sustaining of world economic activity were given priority.

With the Baker initiative, there has been a new attitude towards conditionality and the priorities of borrowing countries' adjustment policies. The Fund's managing director, in an address in November 1985, noted that 'an appropriate adjustment strategy must pay attention to the form as well as the size of external adjustment so that growth – which is so vital to the stamina needed for adjustment – does not suffer.' This implied not only a greater role for the World Bank, but more flexible conditions for the Fund's own lending. The first practical result was seen in the 18-month US$1.5bn 'stand-by' agreement signed with Mexico in July 1986: this took a more accommodating line on the budget deficit (apparently accepting the argument that the high peso cost of government debt-servicing made the IMF's earlier target for reducing the budget deficit unrealistic); it accepted economic growth as a policy target; and it agreed to provide compensatory finance should the price of oil fall below US$9 a barrel, while reducing facilities should it rise above US$14. Compensatory funds for public-sector investment would be released if growth targets for 1987–8 of 3–4 per cent did not seem likely to be achieved in 1987. The package was to be reinforced by World Bank lending of nearly US$2bn, well above the level previously envisaged for the period. The subsequent bank rescheduling followed this precedent by providing for additional contingency funding, linked – with various provisos – to export performance and economic growth.

Apart from the terms themselves, an important aspect of the new IMF approach is the psychological benefit to debtors, the greater political 'saleability' in the borrowing country, and no doubt an improvement in the image of the Fund in the developing world. Although Mexico's needs were particularly clamant, with a prospective loss of perhaps as much as 40 per cent of its export revenue because of the precipitate fall in the price of oil, a precedent for other countries entering into agreement with the Fund must have been created: if fluctuations in the price of oil can be taken into account for Mexico, then why not grain for Argentina? How the new conditionality will work in practice has yet to be seen; the criteria for success under the old and more stringent conditions were more closely interrelated and easier to monitor. Now that growth has been brought into the equation, overall progress in carrying out the terms of an agreement may be more difficult to measure.

Even if, with the involvement of the World Bank in the adjustment process, two Washington agencies are now cooperating much more closely than in the past, the old distinction between adjustment finance and development finance remains, and the IMF seems likely to continue to resist the 'prolonged use of its funds', which it has always seen as inconsistent with its role. A modest exception has been made with the creation of a new Structural Adjustment Facility, from which the first loan – to Burundi – was made in August 1986, in conjunction with other loans from the World Bank and bilateral aid donors; policy targets relate to economic growth, as well as balance of payments and debt. The scale is small – SDR20m for the IMF's own contribution – and although the scheme should be helpful to small African debtors, there is no intention of applying it on a wider scale.

The World Bank

Under the Baker initiative, the World Bank is cast for a much more dynamic role than it has hitherto played in resolving the problems thrown up by the debt crisis. Its approach to developing country finance had already undergone a significant change of thrust in the early 1980s, and the scale of its operations in these new directions will now be increased – for the benefit of major debtors and others – in the new era of 'adjustment-cum-growth'. In the 1970s the World Bank had modified its project lending, hitherto directed mainly to the economic infrastructure, to include agriculture, rural development, education, health and other projects that were designed to have a more immediate impact in meeting 'basic needs' and alleviating poverty. In the 1980s, as viable projects became more difficult to identify, local governments faced increasing budgetary constraint in meeting their share of the costs, and shortage of foreign exchange made quicker disbursement of loans more desirable, the World Bank moved into programme lending in the form of Structural Adjustment Loans (SALs) and, increasingly since 1984, the less ambitious 'sectoral adjustment' loans. Disbursements under both these kinds of loan are linked to reforms in administration, institutions and economic policies, with the aim of increasing efficiency in the allocation of resources and removing obstacles to development and growth. They therefore focus particularly on such areas as pricing, subsidies and trade liberalization – as does the IMF in its general policy recommendations.

A major recipient of SALs has been Turkey, which received a series of five between 1980 and 1984, totalling US$1.6bn, about one-third of all the SALs granted by the Bank in that period. Sectoral adjustment loans have been distributed more widely, and are replacing the more ambitious SALs. In 1985–6, sectoral adjustment lending amounted to about 14 per cent of all World Bank commitments. When, in addition to these types of adjustment loan, those granted for sectoral investment and maintenance or provided to intermediaries for on-lending are included, the proportion of loans that is in some way policy-oriented will be much higher, and especially for the Baker countries. For Latin America in particular, policy-based loans and those with a 'strong sector policy content' will rise in the current year to about 40 per cent of a substantially larger total loan commitment.

Loans are linked to a diverse range of policy measures. Recent lending of this type includes US$250m to Chile to support trade liberalization, taxation and fiscal reform, with a further US$100m in an 'Industrial Restructuring Loan' to support reforms in the banking system and the financial restructuring of individual industrial firms. A loan of US$100m to Ecuador is described as supporting policy measures that will curtail the government's participation in certain public enterprises, relax trade restrictions and liberalize agricultural pricing policies. For Brazil a US$500m 'Credit and Marketing Reform Loan' is linked to agricultural policy, including the reduction of rural credit subsidies, and a loan for Argentina is related to a shift in the system of taxation away from export taxes to a system based on land values, together with a liberalization of imports of agricultural machinery.

Loans of these kinds are disbursed in 'tranches', of which the second is conditional on performance; on some loans to smaller countries the second tranche has been withheld. Conditionality as applied to World Bank loans is clearly a different matter from the conditionality attached to IMF stand-bys. Weak conditionality, with few or vaguely defined policy changes demanded, or linking to changes that would in any case have come about, would make a loan seem little more than general balance-of-payments support, and some observers see them in this light. On the other hand, insistence on far-reaching reforms might be seen as the imposition of an economic development strategy that could arouse resentments, as IMF programmes have so often done in Latin America in the past. The questions are complex; the nature of the World Bank's involvement must clearly depend very largely on the nature of the economy being supported and the sophistication of its administration.[18]

In addition to its role as provider of finance, increasingly on policy-related terms, the operations of the World Bank have a further relevance for creditor banks by inducing them to lend, by means of co-financing arrangements, to developing countries which, though they may still be creditworthy, have potential balance-of-payments problems that may also suggest caution. If the result is to obviate the need for rescheduling, it is clearly to the banks' advantage: this seems to have been the case with Hungary in 1984, when the banks put up US$230m of a US$400m package arranged by the World Bank, plus a further co-financing in 1985, when the banks contributed about two-thirds of a total of US$1.2bn. In the latter year the World Bank also guaranteed half of the US$300m loan to Chile that formed part of the banks' overall new money package amounting to US$1.1bn. More recently the World Bank has co-financed and guaranteed part of the contingency credit to Mexico extended by the commercial banks under the arrangements negotiated in late 1986.

Co-financing between the World Bank and other lenders has of course been practised since long before the debt crisis; the commercial banks first became involved in 1974. Other co-financing partners, and for much larger amounts in total, have been bilateral official aid and export-credit organizations. The system for World Bank co-financing with private commercial banks, as modified in 1983, provided for two interrelated loan operations: an 'A' loan provided entirely by the World Bank, and a 'B' loan provided by the commercial banks, in which the World Bank also participates, by taking the later maturities of the loan, by guaranteeing such maturities or by accepting a contingent liability to take over the 'stretched-out' maturities that may be created when a ceiling is set on annual repayments. (The Paraguayan loan of 1984, already referred to, is the only example of the last type.)

How far these mechanisms will generate a greater flow of commercial bank lending to developing countries than would otherwise have taken place, and particularly in respect to really spontaneous lending to the rescheduling countries, has yet to be seen. However, a co-financed loan of US$90m, split equally between a group of commercial banks and the World Bank, arranged for Uruguay in 1986 and described as the first voluntary lending to any Latin American country since the debt crisis, was reported to have been oversubscribed. In principle, there seems no reason why World Bank policy-oriented loans cannot be co-financed as well as project loans. But the banks cannot abandon their own judgment on creditworthiness, and the arrangements made in 1983 still do not absolve them from risk. A guarantee against default is not a guarantee against rescheduling. It is not inconceivable that early maturities of a loan could be rescheduled, while the later maturities held by the World Bank were excluded. Co-financed loans contracted before 1983 have in fact been included in reschedulings – for example in the case of the

Philippines – and bank regulators appear to have different views as to whether co-financed loans merit any preferential status in relation to reserve requirements. Bankers in the USA and elsewhere have urged that the whole procedure for co-financing should be strengthened by effective cross-default clauses that would oblige the World Bank to impose sanctions if the commercial portion fell into arrears, but it seems unlikely that the Bank could ever accept this, especially since it regards guarantees as a call on capital to the same extent as loans.

Besides its mainstream operations – summarized above in so far as they relate to the problems of the major indebted countries with which the banks are involved – the World Bank group has other activities that are relevant. Largest of the World Bank's related financial institutions is the International Development Association (IDA), created to provide loans on concessional terms to the poorer developing countries; significant as its operations are for debtors in southern Asia and sub-Saharan Africa, its funds are not by definition available to any of the highly indebted bank borrowers, all of which, even Bolivia, are in terms of income above the cut-off point.

The activities of the International Finance Corporation (IFC), being specifically oriented towards the development of the private sector, have a particular relevance for the middle-income countries that have also been the largest borrowers from commercial sources. The IFC promotes the creation or expansion of industrial enterprises by providing loan or equity capital, in conjunction with funds raised from domestic and foreign lenders and investors, and is active as well in finding ways of developing local capital markets. It has also established investment funds that could perform a useful function in attracting portfolio capital investment in developing countries that have sufficiently developed securities markets, such as Brazil and Mexico and others in Asia, on the pattern of that set up for South Korea, as well as providing a vehicle for the return of flight capital. A new 'Emerging Markets Growth Fund' began operation in 1986 with a capital of US$50m, placing shares initially with a small number of institutional investors who were prepared to diversify into high-risk, high-return areas; the IFC hopes that the Fund may grow to US$500m. A further initiative in 1986 is the announcement of a 'Guaranteed Recovery of Investment Principal' scheme that will create a new financial instrument, managed by the IFC, designed to protect foreign equity investment from capital loss over a specified period; individual investments of up to US$100m may be eligible.

Another initiative in the foreign investment area that has made progress is the proposal to establish a Multilateral Investment Guarantee Agency (MIGA) that would operate under the aegis of the World Bank. Its purpose is to complement present activities of the World Bank itself, the IFC, national investment insurance schemes and others in encouraging increased international investment in developing countries. The agency would issue guarantees to investors against non-commercial risk – such as transfer of earnings and capital, expropriation, war and civil disturbance and breach of contract – as well as providing technical and advisory services and consultation on investment policies and programmes. With the signature of the USA in June 1986 (following the Netherlands, Italy, Canada and the UK), the minimum commitment of five developed and fifteen developing countries, representing over 40 per cent of the authorized capital of US$1.1bn, has been obtained. Parliamentary or congressional ratification of the commitment to subscribe to the agency will no doubt be required in many countries, though this should not be difficult, even in the USA, because of the relatively low level of paid-in subscriptions. But with many matters still to be settled at the conference set up to formulate its regulations and policies – will it, for example, cover royalty payments? – it is unlikely to come into operation before the second half of 1987.

There is a considerable divergence of views as to how far investment guarantee schemes actually generate additional investment: this is not measured by the number of investments that are registered under such schemes. But, as noted earlier, it is important at the present time that all positive ideas that might help to encourage equity capital inflows and generally improve the climate for international investment should be put into effect.

The Inter-American Development Bank (IDB)

Of the regional development banks, the one whose activities are most significant in the context of the Baker initiative is the IDB. To increase its lending above the current level of about US$3.0bn a year will require an increase in capital, and there are some differences on policy with the non-regional members, who contribute most of its hard-currency resources. The IDB has always been more sympathetically inclined towards its developing country members and less responsive to its principal shareholder than the World Bank. Its lending is largely project-oriented, though much is directed to the social infrastructure, and it has always resisted policy conditionality in lending. Since the onset of the debt crisis it has introduced some new lending programmes: a Special Operating Programme to help countries that might have difficulty in completing projects, by accelerated disbursements and other means; an Intermediate Financing Facility to subsidize interest-rate relief for some of its poorer members; and an Industrial Recovery Programme providing loans akin to the World Bank's SALs but in one tranche and without the same insistence on policy reforms. The reference in the Baker initiative to the need for the IDB to strengthen its lending procedures implied that they should become more like those of the World Bank, with a progressive increase in lending in the form of conditional policy-linked loans of the SAL and sectoral adjustment type. Agreement between the IDB and its non-regional shareholders on these and other matters will determine the size of the Seventh General Increase in Resources and hence the amount available for lending in 1987–90. On a reasonably optimistic view, it may over the four-year period increase the level of its annual loan authorizations by about 10 per cent.

B. OECD governments

How quickly individual debtor countries will be able, under more liberal refinancing arrangements, to achieve a significant improvement in both their external accounts and their growth performance will clearly depend on the structure of their economies, their capacity for export diversification and the political will that is applied to bringing about economic reform. For them all, much will depend on trends in the world economy that are outside their control: the rate of growth in OECD countries, which provide the bulk of debtor-country export markets, commodity prices and interest rates. Inevitably, the broad lines of economic policy in the industrial countries are determined by considerations other than the needs of the debtors. To sustain their own economic growth is the most important permanent contribution they can make, and to keep down, and if possible reduce, interest rates the most immediate way to bring relief to the debtors: put simply, a one per cent change in average interest rates paid by Brazil and Mexico on bank debt makes a difference to the balance of payments of the order of US$700–800m a year.

Of policy measures in OECD countries that are more specifically related to debtor country needs, a continued resistance to demands for trade protection is clearly of the highest importance, especially in the USA, which provides the largest market for manufactured exports from western hemisphere debtor countries. A further question is whether the industrial countries will increase official funding of debtors. Budgetary constraints seem likely to continue to inhibit any substantial increase in bilateral aid – nor does it perhaps have the same moral imperative as in early post-imperial years. As noted earlier, the UK, Germany and other countries have written off substantial amounts of government loans to the poorer debtors. These countries have, however, contracted relatively little bank debt, and their debt problems are not also problems for their creditors.

For debtor countries not in this group, the financing contribution from OECD governments must continue to take the form of guarantees for export credits and expanding the resources of the multilateral agencies. As noted earlier, the 'Paris Club' of official export-credit agencies has carried out substantial refinancing operations for indebted countries – some US$36bn for over 30 countries between 1983 and 1985. With an efficient, though ad hoc, administrative framework, the member governments appear usually to reach agreement – or so it seems to the outside world – among themselves and with the debtors more easily than do the banks, though the Paris Club approach is fairly rigid. It does not anticipate problems; it waits for a debtor country to announce that it cannot pay. It insists more absolutely than the banks on an IMF programme as a condition of rescheduling, and doubts as to effective medium-term monitoring of performance are said to have inhibited it in carrying out more multi-year reschedulings. Unlike the banks, it does not provide new money, and they have often criticized it on these grounds; but, against this, it does capitalize interest. Recent terms seem to have been fairly generous: the rescheduling for Mexico reported in September 1986 covered 1986–8 maturities and 60 per cent of interest for a total of US$1.8bn over ten years, with six years of grace.

To provide 'new money' or its equivalent in the form of a specific amount of financing guarantees over a future period would in any case be difficult, since the agencies respond essentially to exporters' demand, which cannot be foreseeable or evenly divided between member countries. Export-credit agencies can, however, move more quickly to restore medium-term cover after a rescheduling – the USA and UK are said to be aligning their policies in this respect with the aims of the Baker initiative – and coordinate their policies more closely. There is a parallel with the policy decision on the part of the banks as to whether increased lending to a rescheduled debtor does improve the quality of the existing portfolio. The practice of the export-credit agencies in the matter of cover is certainly seen by banks as an indicator of creditworthiness. The agencies have a considerable experience of co-financing with the World Bank, and such operations with the Bank's policy-related loans may help to stimulate commercial bank lending to the rescheduling countries. The export-credit agencies are themselves under financial constraints, as rescheduling has impaired their cash flow and required them to call on government funds.

The role of industrial country governments in relation to the multilateral agencies is, or should be, straightforward: to ensure that they have sufficient resources to carry out their allotted task. Whatever reservations there might be about the proper role of commercial banks and export-credit agencies in providing medium- to long-term finance, that is the *raison d'être* of the World Bank and the regional development banks. The World Bank was created as the International Bank for Reconstruction and Development, and its present task in relation to the indebted developing countries has just those purposes. An increase in the capital of the Bank will need to be considered in 1987: a rise of between US\$30bn and US\$80bn is understood to be the Bank's own target range, and it would probably be satisfied with US\$50bn (against a present capital of US\$80bn).

European finance ministers have agreed on the need for a capital increase. Attitudes in the USA are more equivocal: in principle, with the rapprochement between the Bank and the US government over the past year and the leading role ascribed to the Bank under the Baker initiative, it is difficult to see why there should be official opposition to an increase in capital, even though the US, under normal arrangements, would have to subscribe, if not pay in, about one quarter of the increase. Even with government support, a lengthy process of congressional approval could be required in view of US politicians' habitual suspicion of any use of public money that might be interpreted as 'bailing out the banks'. An increase in the shareholding of Japan would seem to offer the readiest means of mobilizing some of that country's increasing surplus for development assistance and easing the recovery path of the debtor countries. To raise the shareholding of Japan more than proportionately would decrease that of the USA, which would probably not wish to see its shareholding fall below the 20 per cent level and a reduction in its influence over the Bank's lending operations. Whether the Bank's charter should be amended to allow it to gear up its capital by more than the very conservative 1:1 ratio is a more difficult question. It has often been raised, but the Bank itself has never supported the idea, on the grounds that it might impair its high standing on international capital markets; it would probably argue that the present time of substantial change in the nature of its lending is not appropriate for any dilution of its capital base.

Over the past year or so, and since they welcomed the Baker initiative, OECD governments – collectively as well as individually – seem rather to have distanced themselves from the question of developing country debt. There have been other preoccupations at economic summits – notably the imbalance between the OECD countries themselves. The world economic environment that the OECD governments create must in a large measure influence the ability of major debtor countries to carry out the debt-servicing plans that they and their creditors devise. OECD countries are the principals; the developing countries reactive. If the consequence of US and other OECD government action is to raise interest rates and bring about an economic recession, as in the early 1980s, other countries must adjust: how far this puts an obligation on OECD governments is a question outside the scope of this study. Their minimum contribution must be to keep markets open for developing country exports; to maintain, if they cannot increase, official financial flows; and to enable the multilateral agencies to carry out the central role that has been assigned to them.

7
PROSPECTS AND POLICIES

The achievements of the past four years should not be underrated: the maintenance of a dialogue, in all but a few cases, between debtors and creditors; the rescheduling of US$140bn of bank debt – perhaps the largest and most complex series of financial negotiations that has ever taken place; and a notable economic adjustment effort on the part of most debtor countries, which for the fifteen heavily indebted states produced a turn-round in the balance of payments of US$50bn on current account. A new and more constructive approach to the problems of the most heavily indebted countries has been outlined and its implementation begun.

Given the attitudes and interests of the various parties, it would be difficult to formulate any practicable approach to the debt problem that would differ basically from the Baker initiative: to stimulate the flow of medium- and long-term capital to debtor countries; to utilize more of the resources of the multilateral agencies and disburse them more quickly; to recognize that economic growth must be pursued simultaneously with, and not be subordinated to, stabilization; and to encourage economic reforms that will increase efficiency and strengthen export capacity. These reforms are directed at weaknesses in the economies of debtor countries that in many cases are of long duration and are themselves partly responsible for the severity of their debt problems: the excessive growth of the public sector, whose chronic deficits have been a prime cause of inflation, and a relatively poor export performance, particularly by Latin American countries, whose share of world exports and of those of the developing countries as a group fell consistently over three decades from 1950.

This does not mean that the debt problem is much nearer to finding its 'solution'. Indeed, no general solution in the sense of disposing of the problem is within the realm of practical politics: there is no organization, or group of countries or institutions, that is willing to bear the cost of the sort of funding exercise that would be required to consolidate past indebtedness and permit current transactions to be carried on unhampered by the legacy of the past. Short of the universal solution, the case-by-case approach is the only viable one, and it is perhaps by bilateral rather than multilateral arrangements that some kind of debt consolidation might eventually be achieved for certain countries. Meanwhile, if the burden of debt cannot be removed, the task is to make it tolerable.

How successfully the Baker formula is going to work in practice for the largest debtor countries has yet to be seen. The collapse of oil prices has made necessary a renegotiation of the MYRA for Mexico, with further extension of maturities and new money in both conventional and new contingent forms, and a rather tightly drawn interdependence between disbursements of the banks and the multilateral agencies. In late 1986 the renegotiation of terms of the Venezuelan MYRA was still uncompleted, as were the reschedulings for Nigeria and the Philippines. Brazil's refusal to accept an IMF programme, if maintained, seemed likely to create problems in reaching a long-term agreement with both the Paris Club and the banks, while Argentina had not yet concluded its 'stand-by' agreement with the IMF (announced in January 1987). The banks' rescheduling teams seemed likely to remain fully occupied well into 1987.

When all these and other arrangements are fully in place, how long will be needed before it is apparent to both creditors and debtors that the so far continually receding goal of a return to creditworthiness is at last in sight? Clearly much will depend on the world economic environment in which debtor countries will have to carry out their policies of adjustment to lower real incomes.

A major influence on the balance of payments of the debtors and on their relative economic performance will continue to be exercised by commodity prices, and especially that of oil. The collapse of oil prices in early 1986 radically altered the outlook for Mexico,

Venezuela, Nigeria and Ecuador, among the Baker Fifteen, as well as for Algeria and Indonesia, all of which depended for over 50 per cent of their export earnings on petroleum, and in the case of Venezuela, Nigeria and Algeria for 90 per cent. Three other countries, Colombia, Peru and Bolivia, were adversely affected to a lesser degree. The remainder either are approximately self-sufficient in oil, like Argentina, or benefited from the fall as importers, notably Brazil. The immediate effects of a fall in oil prices are not symmetrical as between oil-exporting and oil-importing developing countries, because they are felt severely by the smaller number of exporters, owing to their excessive dependence for foreign exchange and budgetary revenue on this one commodity, while the benefits are diffused through the much larger number of importers.[19] This is not inconsistent with attributing to the oil price rises of the 1970s the major influence in building up the debt problem: the proportionate increases were then larger, and whereas oil importers have made significant progress in economizing in the use of energy, the major oil exporters had become more dependent on their leading export, and more countries have invested resources in the business of exporting oil.

Medium-term forecasts of commodity prices are notoriously fallible. At some point – but perhaps not until well into the 1990s – the pressure on oil prices will swing to the demand side, but for some years it seems that supplies and potential supplies will exceed demand so that the success of OPEC in keeping some control over its members' output will remain a major determinant of prices. Shocks to the world economic system, such as that produced by violent movements in the price of oil, are always harmful. Though a fall in the price of oil raises incomes and demand in the industrial countries and is thus favourable to world economic growth, the direct destabilizing effect on the balance of payments of particular countries is more immediately apparent. The advantage of price stability seems now to have become quite generally recognized on both sides: Saudi Arabia has made clear that it does not wish the price to rise much above US$18 a barrel in the medium term – a level that would curb the development of the more expensive oilfields outside OPEC and the switch to alternative fuels, but provide members with an income to which they could adjust; the governments of Western industrial countries, on the other hand, would not welcome a fall in prices that threatened the viability of their own oil

73

industries and a return to profligacy in the use of fuel. With some non-OPEC producers willing to collaborate, there might possibly emerge an informal acceptance of a desirable range of oil prices between US$15 and US$20 a barrel.

Stabilization of oil prices in such a range would no doubt provide the best environment for the successful management of the debt problem. The outlook for other commodity prices is not particularly encouraging; non-oil-exporting developing countries have suffered a cumulative adverse movement in the terms of trade of about 13 per cent between 1979 and 1985. Apart from the cyclical influences on agricultural commodities, the longer-term factors that have tended to depress commodity prices – ample supplies, technological changes that limit the growth of demand in industrial countries and a relatively slow rate of overall economic growth in those countries – seem likely to persist into the medium term. The fundamental weakness of the market for many commodities has been seen in their muted reaction to the fall in the value of the US dollar, the currency in which they are normally quoted. Even if developing country export prices for both commodities and manufactures do rise in the medium term in line with the moderate rate of inflation expected in industrial countries, it seems doubtful whether the former will recoup their earlier losses in the terms of trade.

Any assessment of the combined effect of these various influences – the supply of external finance, export demand, terms of trade and interest rates – must be fallible. The IMF has drawn up a medium-term scenario with variants; how this might work out in the base case for the fifteen heavily indebted countries is shown in Table 7. The picture is not very encouraging: on an assumption of a growth in external borrowing of 9 per cent a year from official and 3 per cent from private sources, moderate economic growth rates – 3.3 per cent in 1987, rising to 4.2 per cent a year in 1988–91 – are foreseen, but there is only a small improvement in debt service/export and debt/GDP ratios. Meanwhile, the small deficit on current account implies a continued large surplus on goods and services other than the service of capital, so that these countries continue to make substantial net transfers of resources abroad.

Such transfers have generally been regarded as unnatural in the context of developing country finance; these countries are conventionally supposed to be by definition net capital importers and therefore to run deficits on current account, and to continue the

Table 7 Heavily indebted countries: debt ratios and balance of payments, 1981–91 (%)

	1981	1982	1983	1984	1985	1986	1987	1989	1991
Debt/exports	201.4	269.2	289.5	270.3	285.1	324.8	311.0	249.2	216.7
Debt/GDP	35.0	42.2	48.0	46.3	45.7	46.6	45.4	—	—
Debt service/exports	38.8	49.4	41.6	40.8	40.0	47.4	44.7	44.5	36.7
of which:									
Interest	22.6	30.7	29.9	29.0	28.1	28.1	24.0	22.9	19.7
Amortization	16.2	18.6	11.7	11.8	11.9	19.3	20.7	21.6	16.9
Current-account balance									
(US$ bn)	−50.0	−50.1	−13.8	−0.9	−0.1	−7.3	−5.1	−2.7	0.2

Source: IMF, *World Economic Outlook*. April and October 1986.
Debt = long- and short-term, except in the case of amortization, which applies to long-term debt only.
Exports = goods and services.

process up to a point where they generate sufficient domestic savings to finance investment. But spontaneous capital movements do of course depend on the rate of return on the investment, and reverse transfers are implicit in all such movements. They are acceptable if, for consumers, they provide present satisfaction deemed worth the burden of future repayment; they are acceptable to investors who aim to place their borrowed funds where they can earn a rate of return higher than the cost. For a sovereign borrower the question is more complicated: whether foreign borrowing increased consumer satisfaction, helped to feed the flight of capital abroad, or actually increased investment rates is unlikely anywhere to be clearly demonstrable. At least it is true that large-scale borrowing during the period 1974–82 did not necessarily lead to a debt crisis: in this respect the example of South Korea is instructive.[20] Whether reverse transfers of the order of 3 per cent a year or more of GDP will in practice prove tolerable to the heavily indebted countries is one of the imponderables and is essentially a political question. Clearly, such transfers are more tolerable in a context of economic growth that makes possible a gradual recovery in living standards and where taxation policies achieve an equitable sharing of the burden.

The commercial banks' own likely contribution to debtor country financing during the period of 'adjustment-cum-growth' is difficult to assess. They have taken on no specific commitment to increase their lending to problem countries; many, and especially the smaller, banks seem to feel that they have made a sufficient contribution by participating in rescheduling packages and would like to opt out of such arrangements in the future. It is doubtful how far major banks would willingly increase their exposure to the rescheduling countries, even when they have emerged from the stage of requiring concerted lending, at least outside the area of short-term trade finance. Examples that might be classed as truly voluntary lending are too few for generalization. The rebuilding of capital and reserves has not in itself made more attractive further lending to countries on which exposure must still seem in many cases uncomfortably high. The position is even more difficult for banks which have to make provisions against both new and existing loans to certain problem debtors.

In a wider context, the commercial banks' attitude towards lending to developing countries generally seems ambiguous. Certainly they are continuing to carry out lending operations, but the evidence suggests that, with the exception of Japanese banks, they are being very cautious about where they lend and how much they increase their exposure. The adjusted BIS figures quoted in Chapter 5 (summarized in Table 6) show a rise of only about 3 per cent for total international bank claims on non-OPEC developing countries in 1985 – almost entirely in the Far East – and a small decline in the first half of 1986. In the UK the Committee of London and Scottish Bankers has drawn attention to the fact that in 1985 UK bank lending to non-oil developing countries in Africa grew by 11 per cent and lending to Eastern Europe by 15 per cent.[21] The latter must, however, be considered a separate category, and lending to Africa is only some 7 per cent of UK banks' exposure to non-oil developing countries. Total claims of UK-registered monetary institutions, and their branches and subsidiaries world-wide, were in fact almost unchanged between mid-1985 and mid-1986. Data for all US banks show a decline in lending exposure to all developing countries of 7.2 per cent in 1985.

When allowance is made for valuation changes, write-offs, securitization and other factors, it is difficult not to conclude that there is a general disinclination on the part of UK and US banks, which *a fortiori* is likely to be shared by continental European banks, to increase their exposure except perhaps in certain areas of special interest. Against this background, it requires a certain optimism to look for even the modest increase in bank lending to the problem countries that was suggested by Baker. It may well be that if these countries return to creditworthiness, the banks will prefer that they seek their requirements in the securities markets, as Far Eastern borrowers have begun to do. The answer to the question whether the banks have learned a lesson from their international lending experiences over the past fifteen years is that they have probably learned it all too well, at least as far as the developing countries are concerned.[22] The pattern of developing country finance has reverted to something nearer to its historical shape and will no doubt for many years conform more closely to it.

While the debtor countries will have to live with the consequences of their excessive borrowing, the same is true of the lending banks. Whatever policy they may adopt towards new loans for problem debtors – and it is suggested that their engagement looks like being minimal – the overhang of old debt must remain a potential, if gradually attenuating, source of weakness for an indefinite period.

They have built up capital and reserves: in the USA, as noted earlier, capital ratios are now above 6 per cent for all banks; in the UK the weighted average free capital ratios of the clearing banks has risen from 4.2 per cent in 1982 to 7.1 per cent at the end of June 1986. This represents a considerable reduction in the banks' vulnerability in respect to their exposure to the problem debtor countries. The position at the end of 1985 for the main groups of US banks engaged in international lending is shown in Table 8.

Table 8 US banks' exposure to heavily indebted countries (15), end-1985 (US$ bn and percentages)

	Nine money–centre banks	Fourteen other large banks	Others	Total
Total exposure, US$ bn	57.1	15.6	14.4	87.0
(% of total)	(66)	(18)	(17)	(100)
Exposure as % of capital	129	72	32	79
Exposure to largest debtor, US$ bn	15.9	4.7	5.6	23.8
Exposure to largest debtor as % of capital	36	22	12	21

Source: Federal Financial Institutions Examination Council.

The table shows the strong concentration of risk in the money-centre banks, among which the highest individual bank exposure to a single country of the group represented probably over 3 per cent of total assets and over 40 per cent of primary capital. Distribution of risk between individual banks is in fact far from homogeneous. The relatively small commitment of banks in the category of 'other' – numbering about 170 – is notable, and this group has been reducing its collective exposure on developing countries by about 8 per cent a year since 1984. On the assumption that bank capital and assets grow at about the same rate as money GDP, the scale of the problem gradually diminishes, providing that lending to the debtors in question does not increase as fast as domestic lending. If nominal GDP were to grow by 6 per cent a year, the current level of exposure of the nine US money-centre banks would, after five years, still represent 96 per cent of capital and to Brazil alone 27 per cent;[23] after ten years the figures would be 72 per cent and 20 per cent. Even with a 10 per cent annual rise in money GDP and a parallel growth of bank capital, the corresponding figures are 80 per cent and 22 per cent after five years, and 50 per cent and 14 per cent after ten.

Such comprehensive analyses of bank indebtedness to developing countries in relation to capital are not available for countries other than the USA. These figures are of especial significance, however, since they relate to the country whose banks collectively hold a much larger share of developing country debt than any other and are also believed to have made, with few exceptions among the larger banks, a rather low level of provisions against sovereign debt.

How to assess the lenders' vulnerability implied by these figures, and how that vulnerability might be affected by additional lending, must be a continuing and difficult task for the banks and their regulators. The situations of the various debtor countries are unlikely to evolve in parallel: the effectiveness of adjustment policies in bringing about an acceptable level of economic growth, success in diversifying and expanding exports, and above all the political reaction are likely to be very different. The world economic environment, as noted above, seems at best likely to be only moderately helpful. A general collapse of debtor country economies seems unlikely unless there were a world recession of unforeseen severity that would call for emergency action in most areas of economic policy. It is generally accepted, and no doubt with reason, that the authorities in the USA and the UK would not allow a money-centre or clearing bank to collapse – or other authorities a major bank elsewhere – though such assurance, for the 'moral hazard' reason,* is never made explicit.

A more likely scenario is that one or more debtor countries may, over a period of five years or more, fail to find an acceptable 'adjustment-cum-growth' path, and consequently be unwilling or incapable of maintaining a plausible servicing of debt, thus making inevitable greatly increased loan-loss provisions by the banks and eventual write-offs. No doubt the banks and their regulators would find the means to deal with such situations that did not impair the banks' credibility in the market. Because this danger does exist, however, and it is not possible to forecast with assurance which borrowing countries might in the end turn out to be the real long-

*I.e., the risk that assurance of future support may encourage imprudent behaviour or weaken efforts at self-help. 'Moral hazard' has sometimes been invoked as a reason for not offering more generous terms to debtors.

term problem debtors, it would seem prudent for the banks, their regulators and the taxation authorities in countries where provisions against sovereign risk are relatively low, and especially in the USA and UK, to anticipate such an eventuality by increasing their level to somewhere nearer those prevailing in continental Europe.

In any case, to suppose that in the end the banks will emerge from the developing country debt crisis without any appreciable losses would perhaps require on their part a fairly high degree of optimism. Clearly, the bulk of the debt at present owed to banks cannot in any foreseeable circumstances be repaid. The form of indebtedness may change, and conversions may erode it at the margin; but it would be unrealistic to suppose that the exchange of debt for equity, even with the opportunities that may be offered by privatization, and other operations in the secondary market can substantially reduce the amount owed by the major debtor countries. Nor, on any plausible scenario, are today's problem debtors likely to generate such surpluses on current account, or attract such large inflows of non-bank capital, as to make possible not only the payment of interest on, but also a significant amortization of, bank debt. Whether in concerted form or by voluntary lending, the existing debt of even the most economically successful of these countries will be rolled over or replaced.

With regard to many – and perhaps to most – of the problem debtors, the question that must arise for their creditors is not repayment of existing debt but the degree to which it can hold its nominal value. To raise the question is not to be unduly sceptical about the effectiveness of the Baker approach; rather, it is to suggest that if, in the event, it does not produce the required result – the regular servicing of debt within an economic context that is tolerable for debtor countries – some other and more radical approach may become necessary. The problem will then be how to help those countries which do not wish to take the uncertain path of unilateral action to limit debt service, but which, even though willing to cooperate with their creditors, require repeated debt-relief operations.

In such circumstances, it might be appropriate to seek some form of securitization of the long-term debt of countries that are capable of pursuing a reasonably steady course of economic growth and, but for the overhang of old debt, would have a good claim to creditworthiness. For banks in at least some of the creditor countries, the consolidation of old debt into a long-term security at a lower than market yield might eventually seem preferable to affording a comparable relief through increasing their lending exposure in the form of new money under a conventional rescheduling operation. Such a debt consolidation could be offered in the context of a proven ability on the part of the debtor country to cooperate with the multilateral agencies in carrying out a programme of economic reform. Creditor banks would more easily be able to enter into such consolidation arrangements to the extent that they had already made provisions against the debt; cooperation of the bank regulators and of the taxation authorities would of course be indispensable.

Debt consolidation of this kind could be undertaken bilaterally by the banks based in particular countries without infringing the rights of other parties, though it would break the common front that has so far been maintained by the creditors. Once conceded, a debt consolidation on concessional terms would no doubt have a strong 'demonstration effect' that could only with difficulty be resisted. If seen as a reasonable alternative to an indefinite prolongation of present rescheduling arrangements, it would not necessarily affect adversely the banks' standing in the market. Some such series of initiatives, though unlikely to be undertaken in the immediate future, might eventually be seen as a mutually acceptable way to resolve a large part of the developing country debt problem; it would certainly be preferable to a seemingly endless series of negotiations that would inhibit long-term policy-making on both sides.

NOTES

1 See David F. Lomax, *The Developing Country Debt Crisis* (Basing-stoke, Macmillan, 1986), pp. 20ff, for an array of relevant quotations.

2 These percentages are derived from BIS figures and exclude lending through offshore centres, which also increased rapidly during the period but was not brought properly into the reporting system until 1983. Claims on developed countries exclude inter-bank loans.

3 The relative importance of the rise in oil prices, other terms of trade effects, the fall in demand for exports due to the recession, and the rise in interest rates on the accumulation of developing country debt have been estimated by William R. Cline in *International Debt and the Stability of the World Economy* (Institute for International Economics, Washington, DC, 1983).

4 Lending to Eastern Europe began against a background of détente and a low level of external indebtedness. By 1976 Poland already needed to continue borrowing in order to service existing debt. The position was correctly analysed by Richard Portes among academic economists, but not until the political disturbances of 1980 did the weakness of Poland's economic position become clearly apparent to official and private lenders in the West.

5 If this record were to be maintained, it would justify the much-quoted remark in 1981 of the then chairman of Citicorp, with regard to sovereign lending, that countries do not go bankrupt.

6 IMF, *World Economic Outlook*, April 1986, p. 91.

7 If interest payments fell more than 90 days in arrear, US banks were obliged to take such interest into profits only on a cash, rather than an accrual, basis. After 180 days, loans were classed as 'value-impaired' and required the allocation of loan-loss provisions out of profits.

8 Capitalization would involve absorbing interest payments, due or past due, into the principal amount of the loan and hence making

them eligible for rescheduling. Although a recognized practice in European countries, it was quite unacceptable to US banks. Capitalization of interest had been granted to Nicaragua in 1980, but that country's economic situation was so disastrous that it could not convincingly be cited as a precedent.

9 Brazilian banks had sizeable claims on other developing countries, including rescheduling ones, as well as Poland.

10 What the position was if one of the banks itself failed was later to become a matter of some controversy.

11 Brazil, although still a primary product exporter, was an exception because its large trade in manufactures enabled it to increase exports substantially in 1983 and 1984, so that it was able to eliminate its current-account deficit and resume economic growth more quickly than other major debtor countries.

12 Margins on 'tax-spared' loans were much lower.

13 As noted earlier, comprehensive data on cross-border lending are available only for US and UK banks. Their share of total lending to all developing countries at mid-1986 was about 24 per cent and 11 per cent respectively. The Japanese share may be estimated at about the same as that for the UK. Of the other lenders, France and Germany each account for probably well under 10 per cent of the total, and Switzerland for an even smaller percentage. These proportions will of course vary greatly for individual borrowing countries.

14 See Salomon Brothers Inc., 'A Review of Bank Performance: 1986 Edition'.

15 IMF, *International Capital Markets: Developments and Prospects*, Occasional Paper 43 (Washington, DC, February 1986), p. 46.

16 More limited debt-relief schemes may of course be wholly appropriate for many of the poorest countries, especially in Africa, and OECD countries including the UK have been fairly generous in this respect.

17 Morgan Guaranty, *World Financial Markets*, March 1986.

18 See Joan M. Nelson, 'The Diplomacy of Policy-based Lending', in Richard Feinberg *et al.*, *Between Two Worlds: the World Bank's Next Decade* (Overseas Development Council, Washington, DC, 1986).

19 The developing countries as a group are net oil exporters, including OPEC countries, which should no longer be regarded as falling into a separate category.

20 South Korea, a country with very limited natural resources, is the third largest debtor to the banks. It borrowed heavily to finance investment, and its debt/GDP ratio of 56 per cent in 1985 was higher

than the 46 per cent averaged by the fifteen Baker countries; its debt service/export ratio was, however, much lower – at 21 per cent against 44 per cent for the fifteen. With a 12 per cent growth rate and a probable current-account surplus of at least US$2bn in 1986, it has curtailed external borrowing and built up reserves.

21 'Bank Lending to Developing Countries', Evidence submitted to the Treasury and Civil Service Committee, October 1986.

22 In relation to the 'centrally planned' (i.e. communist) countries, the question looks more open.

23 This is not meant to imply that Brazil is an especially high-risk country; it happens to be the country to which this group of banks has the largest exposure.

Related titles

European Interests in Latin America
Esperanza Durán

Although there are strong historical and cultural links between Western Europe and Latin America, relations between them in the postwar period have not been very significant for either region, economically or politically. Latin America is, however, becoming a more important factor in West European foreign policy and in the context of European/American relations.

This study examines and compares the interests and policies in Latin America of the three most important members of the European Community, West Germany, France and the UK. It deals first with economic relations, notably trade (including arms trade), aid, direct investment and the debt problem. The second part considers the political dimension of European/Latin American relations, and explores the obstacles to greater political cooperation. The conclusions highlight the areas where closer contacts between Latin America and Western Europe are feasible, and the issues on which Western Europe could cooperate in fostering relations with some Latin American countries.

International Economic Policy Coordination
Michael Artis and Sylvia Ostry

National economies have become increasingly interlinked in recent years and are now highly interdependent. Yet governments have made few efforts to coordinate economic policies. This paper begins by describing the ways in which economies are connected through trade and finance, and by outlining the case for coordination as well as the obstacles to it. It then examines the international institutions which were constructed in the postwar period, particularly the IMF, and the reasons for their later difficulties. The experience of recent years is analysed in the light of arguments for floating exchange rates, and the role of existing coordination arrangements (especially economic summits) in coping with current problems, such as the US budget deficit and international debt, are discussed. In conclusion the authors consider the prospects for progress towards a more orderly global economy.

Routledge & Kegan Paul